Richard Wailing, Peter's, Sat 17/2/07

EXETER TO TAVISTOCK

Vic Mitchell and Keith Smith

Middleton Press

Cover picture: The 1.0pm Waterloo to Plymouth passes under the narrow arch at Yeoford behind no. 34057 **Biggin Hill** *on 7th May 1960. The Bulleid Light Pacifics saw widespread service in the West of England for two decades. (S.C.Nash)*

First published February 1996

ISBN 1 873793 69 3

© *Middleton Press 1996*

Design - Deborah Goodridge

Published by Middleton Press
Easebourne Lane
Midhurst
West Sussex
GU29 9AZ
Tel: 01730 813169
Fax: 01730 812601

Printed & bound by Biddles Ltd,
Guildford and Kings Lynn

CONTENTS

37	Bow
103	Brentor
89	Bridestowe
35	Coleford Junction
13	Cowley Bridge Junction
20	Crediton
1	Exeter St. Davids
95	Lydford
86	Meldon Junction
74	Meldon Quarry
83	Meldon Viaduct
16	Newton St. Cyres
43	North Tawton
56	Okehampton
50	Sampford Courtenay
110	Tavistock North
28	Yeoford

ACKNOWLEDGEMENTS

We are very grateful for the assistance received from the many photographic contributors mentioned in the captions and also from P.G.Barnes, R.M.Casserley, K.Catchpole, G.Croughton, E.W.Fry, Mrs S.Grove, M.King, A.Ll.Lambert, N.Langridge, J.S.Petley, Mr D. & Dr.S.Salter, M.Turvey, E.Youldon and our ever helpful wives.

The 1955 BR diagram shows the Southern Region with a wide line and the Western Region with a narrow one.

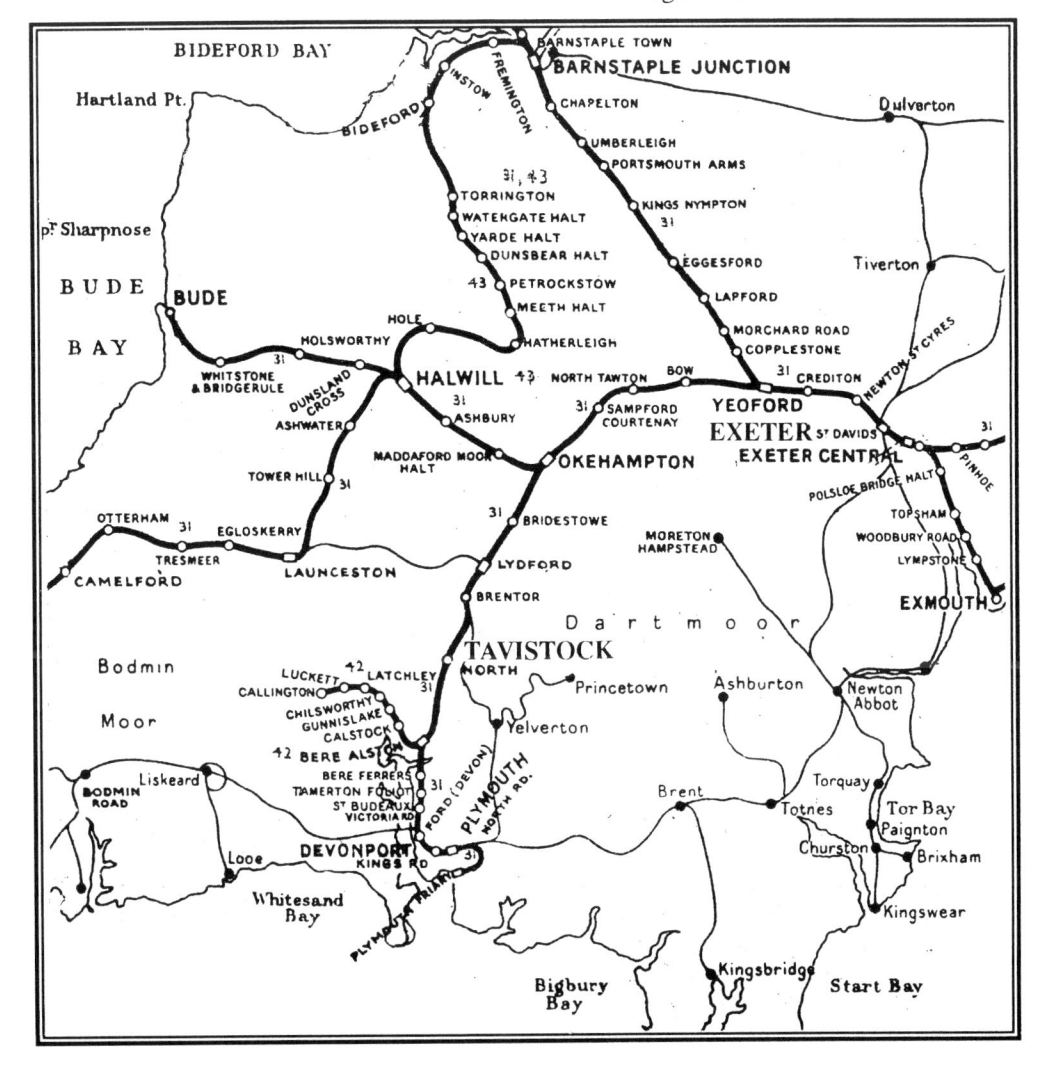

GEOGRAPHICAL SETTING

From the county town and cathedral city of Exeter, the route runs north in the narrow valley of the River Exe for over a mile. From Cowley Bridge Junction it follows the River Yeo and climbs steadily for nearly ten miles before leaving its valley two miles beyond Yeoford. Near Bow, the line dips as it crosses the valley of a different north-flowing River Yeo. There is another dip in the vicinity of North Tawton where the route traverses the valley of the River Taw.

The otherwise almost unbroken climb continues for nearly 30 miles as the line skirts the northern boundary of Dartmoor and reaches its summit one mile west of Meldon Quarry, for long a source of railway ballast. A fifteen mile descent, along the western flank of Dartmoor, brings the railway into Tavistock, an old established market town. It is situated on the River Tavy, the valley of which the line follows for its final two miles.

Most of the route was constructed on shales and grits.

All maps are to the scale of 25 ins to 1 mile, unless otherwise stated. The location maps are at 1 inch to 1 mile and are from the 1930 edition.

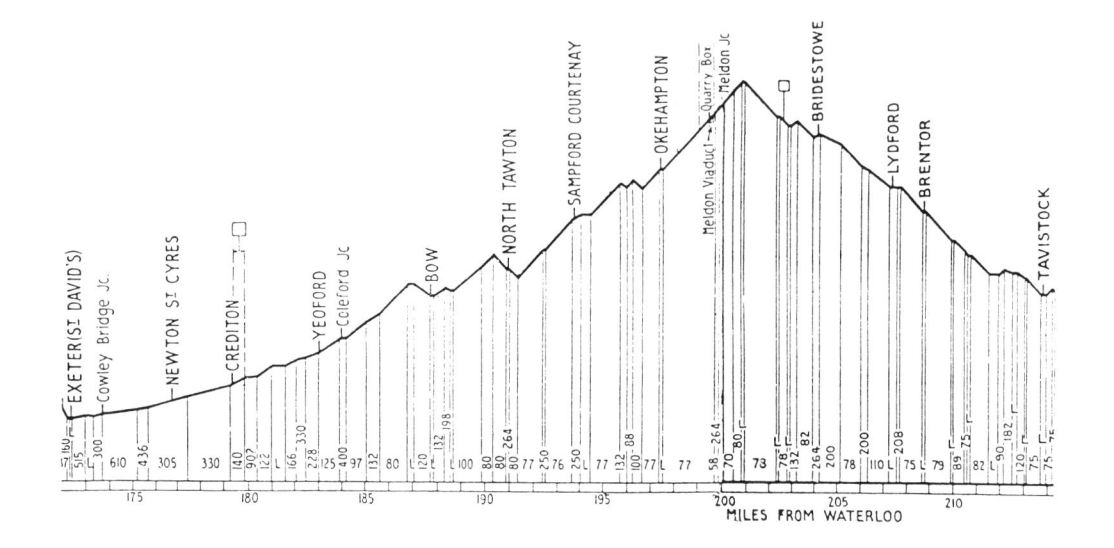

HISTORICAL BACKGROUND

The broad gauge Bristol & Exeter Railway was completed to Exeter on 1st May 1844. It was worked by the Great Western Railway until 1st May 1849 after which date operation was undertaken by the B&ER. The GWR purchased the route on 1st August 1876.

The route south to Teignmouth was opened by the South Devon Railway on 20th May 1846 and was later operated briefly on the atmospheric system. It was worked by the GWR from 1st February 1876 and absorbed by that company on 1st August 1878.

The London & South Western Railway's route from Yeovil to Exeter Queen Street (now Central) opened in 1860 and was extended to St. Davids on 1st February 1862. This was laid to standard gauge.

The Exeter & Crediton Railway's successful Act was passed on 21st July 1845. After protracted arguments, the E&CR was leased to the B&ER and opened on 12th May 1851, having been ready for traffic since January 1847.

The Taw Vale Railway was opened between Barnstaple and Fremington for horse-drawn mineral traffic on 25th April 1848 and for broad gauge passenger services on 1st August 1854. On the same day the Crediton to

Barnstaple section came into use, extension to Bideford following in 1855.

The LSWR already had shares in the Taw Vale Railway but was not able to lease the line until 1862.

The TVR along with the Crediton to Barnstaple section was known collectively as the North Devon Railway. Broad gauge trains between Exeter and Bideford were operated by the NDR itself from 28th July 1855.

From 1st February 1862, the LSWR leased the E&CR and soon added a third rail for its standard gauge trains to enable them to run through from Waterloo. These were extended from Crediton to Bideford on 2nd March 1863. Broad gauge goods trains continued to run to Barnstaple until 1877 and to Crediton until 1892. The GWR retained the right to operate freight trains to Crediton until 1903.

The LSWR opened its line to Plymouth in stages, services commencing to North Tawton on 1st November 1865, to Okehampton Road (Sampford Courtenay) on 8th January 1867, to Okehampton on 3rd October 1871 and to Lydford on 12th October 1874. Here trains joined the GWR's broad gauge branch to Plymouth, a third rail being added. This single line had been opened north to Tavistock in 1859 and was extended to Launceston in 1865.

The LSWR started operating between Okehampton and Holsworthy on 20th January 1879 and completed its own double track route between Lydford and Tavistock (and on towards Plymouth) on 1st June 1890.

The LSWR became part of the Southern Railway in 1923 and this in turn became the Southern Region of British Railways in 1948. In January 1963, Southern Region lines in Devon were transferred to the Western Region.

The stations opened with the line, unless otherwise stated.

Complete closure of the Okehampton - Tavistock - Bere Alston section took place on 6th May 1968 but access to Meldon Quarry was retained. Passenger services between Yeoford and Okehampton were withdrawn on 5th June 1972 (not 5th January as sometimes stated).

PASSENGER SERVICES

These notes refer to the trains running south of Okehampton, the services between Exeter and Yeoford being discussed in the *Exeter to Barnstaple* album. The trains running only between Exeter and Okehampton were very few in number until the 1968-72 period when there were seven trains, weekdays only. The table below shows down train frequency in the summers of selected years.

The "Atlantic Coast Express" ceased to carry a Plymouth portion after 16th June 1963 but through coaches from Waterloo continued to be available on other trains for a short time. The through train from Brighton ran until 4th March 1967.

	WEEKDAYS		SUNDAYS	
	Stopping	Express	Stopping	Express
1869	6	-	-	-
1890	4	3	2	-
1906	6	4	3	2
1914	5	4	2	1
1924	6	5	4	1
1934	5	7	4	2
1938	5	7	4	2
1944	5	3	4	2
1948	4	7	4	2
1954	6	6	4	2
1958	7	6	4	3
1963	7	5	4	3
1965	7	1	4	-
1967	6	-	-	2

EXETER ST DAVIDS

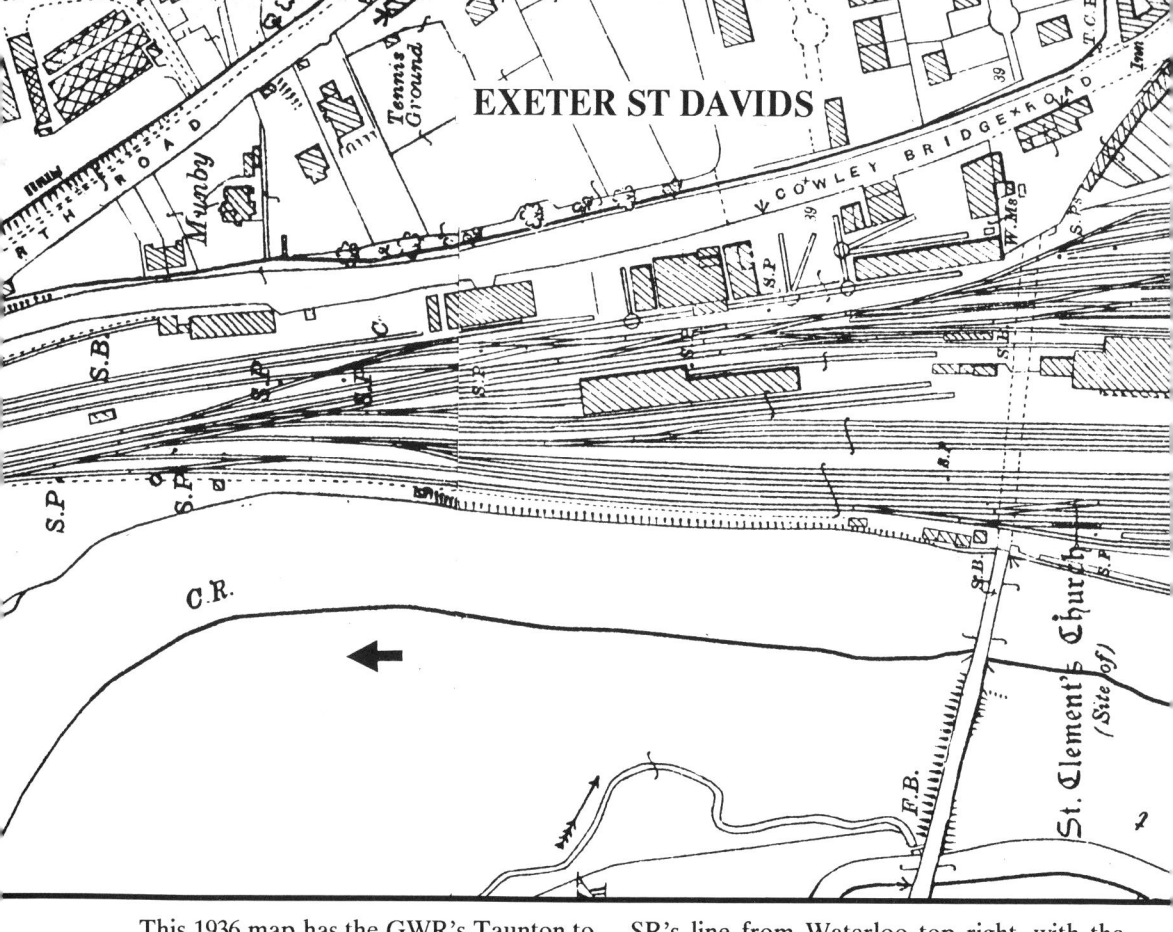

This 1936 map has the GWR's Taunton to Newton Abbot route from left to right and the SR's line from Waterloo top right, with the carriage sheds nearby.

1. The first station had only one platform which was used by both up and down trains. Steady growth in traffic resulted in this fine structure being erected in the early 1860s and four platforms being provided. The roof on the right was replaced by a canopy attached to the front wall in 1939. (Lens of Sutton)

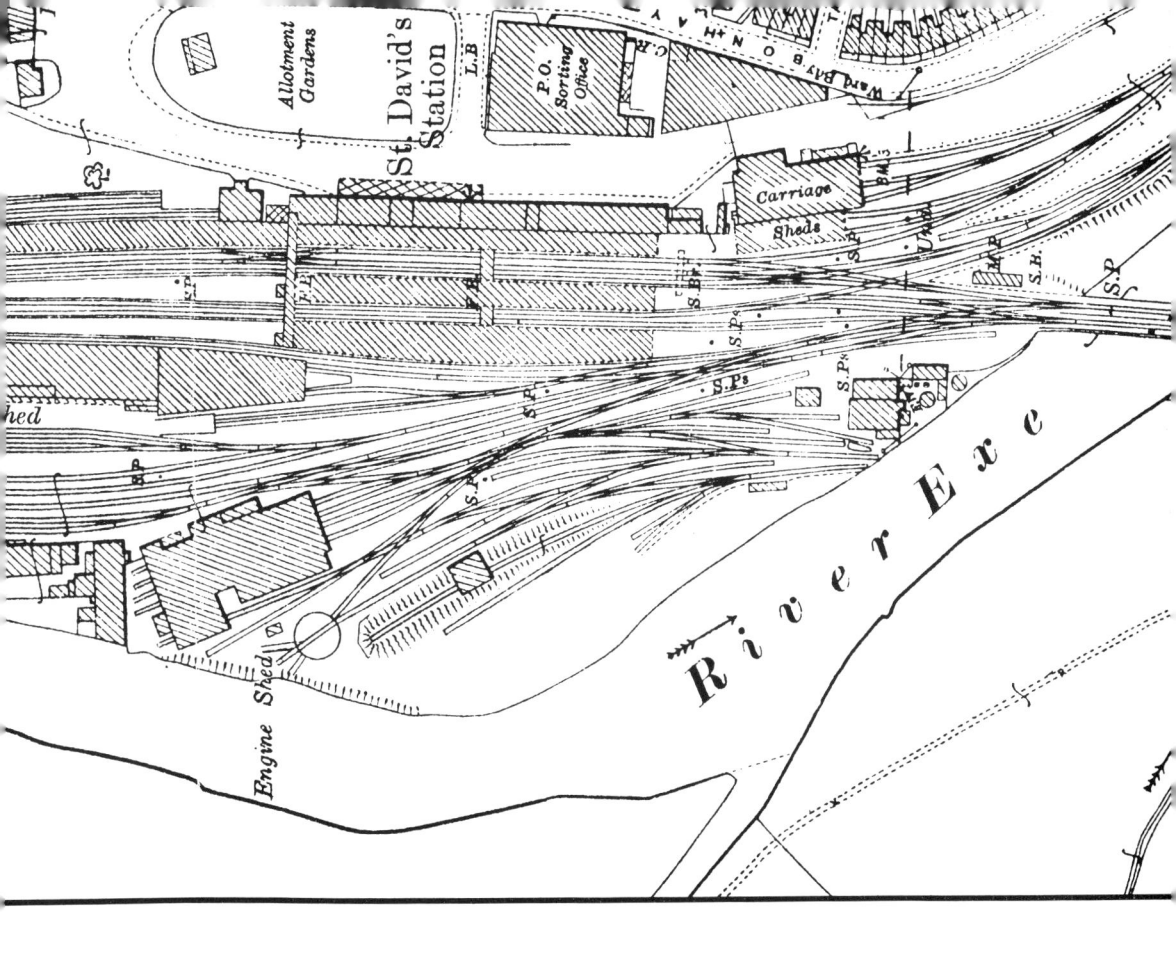

2. Rebuilding again in 1911-14 resulted in five through platforms and a down through line being created. The overall roof was replaced by individual platform canopies. Class N 2-6-0s nos. A857 and A849 are about to start the 1 in 37 climb to Exeter Queen Street in about 1930. (Lens of Sutton)

3. Down SR trains used platform 4 and then the up GWR track north to Cowley Bridge Junction. Here class T9 4-4-0s nos. 117 and 289 wait ready to tackle the long climb to Okehampton. (Lens of Sutton)

4. Locomotives of SR and GWR origin were common but, on 21st October 1950, ex-Plymouth, Devonport & South Western Junction Railway no. 758 *Lord St. Levan* was unusual and was recorded on its way from Plymouth to Exmouth Junction. Partly obscured is no. 5023 *Brecon Castle*. (T.Reardon)

5. Gas for dining cars is being shunted by ex-London, Brighton & South Coast Railway class E1/R 0-6-2T no. 32124 in 1951. The tanks are on an ex-LSWR coach underframe. The 95-lever Middle Box and Red Cow Crossing are also visible. The latter once traversed 14 tracks. (P.Hay)

Other Middleton Press albums to feature Exeter are *Branch Lines to Exmouth, Exeter to Barnstaple, Yeovil to Exeter* **and** *Exeter and Taunton Tramways.*

6. Running over the same crossing on 30th August 1958 is class T9 no. 30726 with the 2.22pm Plymouth Friary to Waterloo. Beyond the goods transfer shed is East Box which opened on 17th June 1942 in connection with a new down goods loop and marshalling yard for wartime traffic. Almost opposite was Riverside Box which came into use on 2nd July 1943. East Box closed on 22nd November 1973 and Riverside Box followed on 5th April 1981. (T.Reardon)

7. Standing on the down main on 19th September 1960 is class N no. 31845 and some fine Devonshire round timber. Such freight trains for the up "Southern" main line had to wait here for a banking engine to come from the siding seen in the centre of the previous picture. (N.L.Browne)

8. To reduce line occupation on busy days, banking engines often returned from Exeter Central attached to the front of down trains. This view from 7th July 1962 shows Z class 0-8-0Ts nos. 30955 and 30956 coupled ahead of "West Country" class 4-6-2 no. 34023 *Blackmore Vale*. The carriage sidings were abolished in July 1969. (H.C.Casserley)

9. Steam vanished from the nearby Exeter shed in 1963 and local services were operated mostly by DMUs thereafter. No. P577 is about to work the 10.55 to Barnstaple on 6th February 1976. The refreshment room (left) dates from 1940. (T.Heavyside)

10. Exeter West Box was nearing the end of its life when no. 33027 was recorded braking empty ballast wagons on 30th May 1984. The box is now a working exhibit at the "Railway Age" at Crewe. The incline to Exeter Central can be seen on the left of the picture. (J.Scrace)

NORTH OF EXETER

11. The extensive Riverside Yard was developed during World War II and subsequently became of great value to freight managers. It was the site of the spectacular Exeter 150 Railfair in May 1994, at which time normal traffic included china clay in transit and Meldon stone for reversal on to the main line. (V.Mitchell)

12. No. 31416 leaves the north end of Riverside Yard on 14th May 1979 with Meldon stone. The down goods loop is above the fifth wagon. (T.Heavyside)

COWLEY BRIDGE JUNCTION

13. The 4.2pm Plymouth to Waterloo train leaves Southern Region rails and runs onto the Western main line on 9th June 1960, headed by no. 34104 *Bere Alston*. The signal box had been extended at its far end in 1943 to accommodate levers to control the points seen in the previous picture. (S.C.Nash)

14. The main line is in the background as no. 31210 turns towards Barnstaple on 12th May 1979. The semaphore signals disappeared when the box closed on 30th March 1985. The line over the three bridges across the the River Exe was singled in 1967 and the one seen in the previous picture was eliminated. The other two were rebuilt as part of a flood relief scheme at that time. (T.Heavyside)

15. A 1992 view of the junction includes the bridge from which the two previous pictures were taken. The branch to Barnstaple was singled as far as Crediton on 16th December 1984. Trains from the branch use the crossover in the foreground. (D.Dornom)

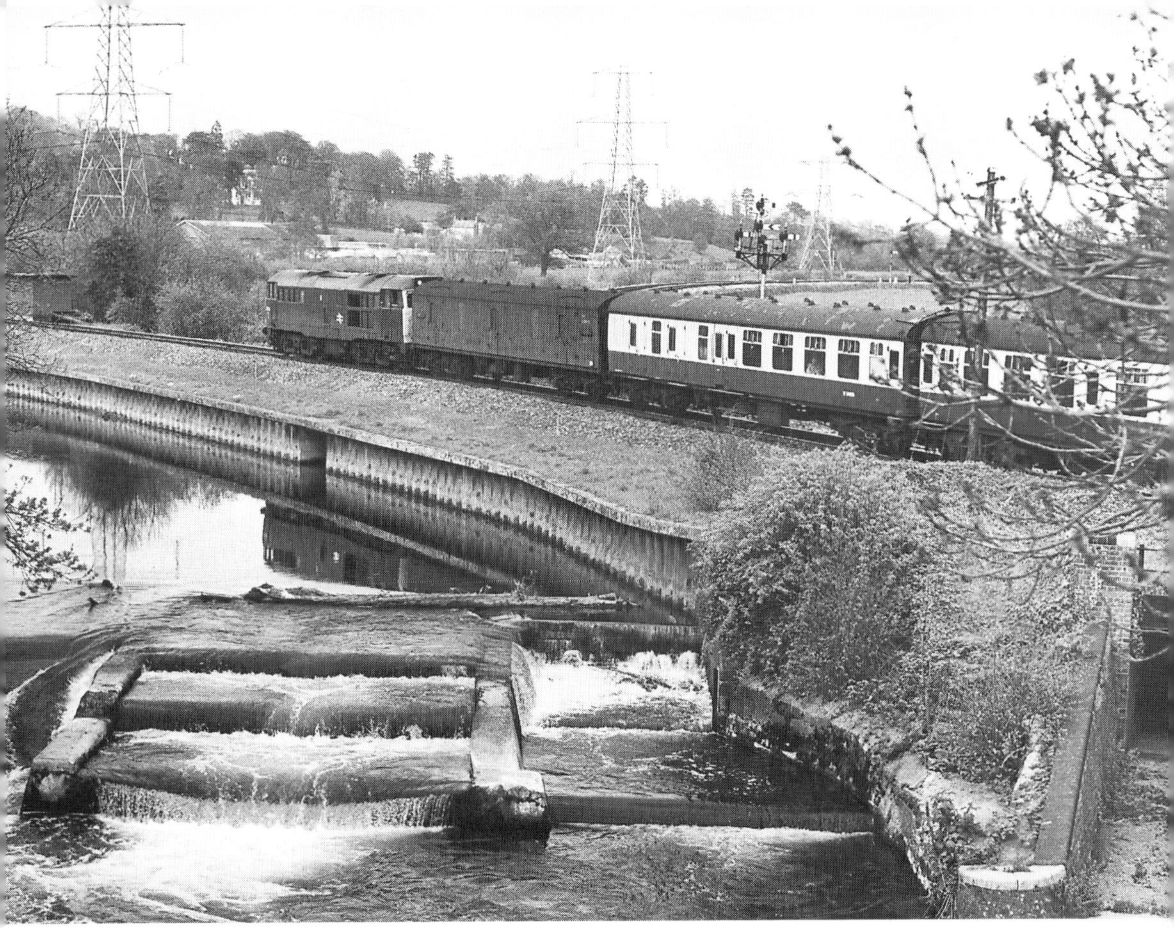

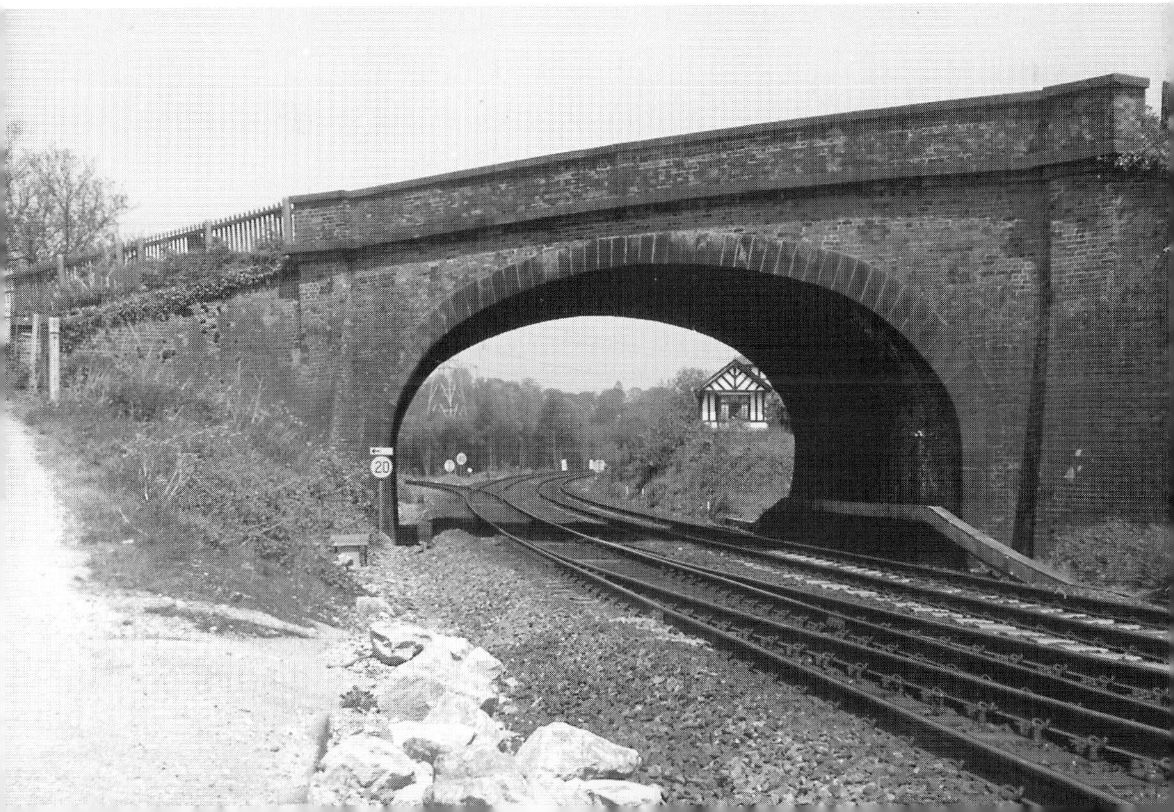
20

NEWTON ST. CYRES

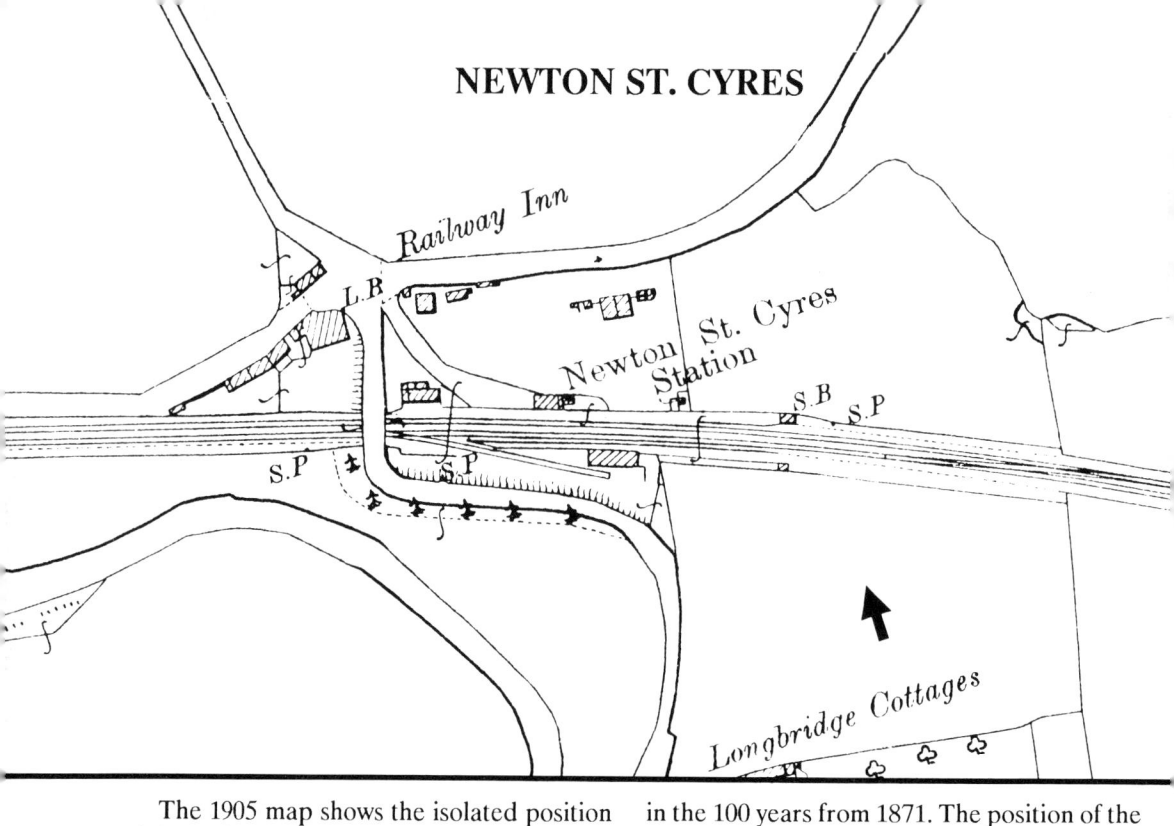

The 1905 map shows the isolated position of the station. It is nearly one mile north of the village, whose population fell from 960 to 830 in the 100 years from 1871. The position of the signal box is marked SB.

16. The nearest hanging sign in this 1965 eastward view is for the ticket office. The station was named simply "St. Cyres" until 1st October 1913. (J.P.Alsop)

17. The buildings were still complete when photographed in 1969, although the signal box had closed on 17th August 1930. A lever frame was in use in the booking office from that date until 31st July 1968. (D.J.Aston)

18. The wide separation of the tracks was a legacy of the broad gauge system which had been doubled here in 1875. It was taken out of use in 1892. DMU no. W51107 approaches the station house on 26th June 1971. (D.Mitchell)

19. No. 33042 passes with a stone train on 10th February 1987. Some unused material is returning to the quarry to avoid splitting the train. A single goods siding had been available for traffic until 12th September 1960 and had been situated on the right of this picture and the left of the previous one. (D.Mitchell)

CREDITON

20. The step in the canopies on the up side (right) indicates the extent to which the platform was widened following the removal of the broad gauge track in the 1890s. The points gave down trains access to the goods yard. (Lens of Sutton)

21. Such patriotic scenes were recorded at many stations in World War I. During WWII this platform received crowds of children evacuated from bomb-prone urban areas. A picture appears in the SR's *War on the Line*, reprinted by Middleton Press. (Lens of Sutton)

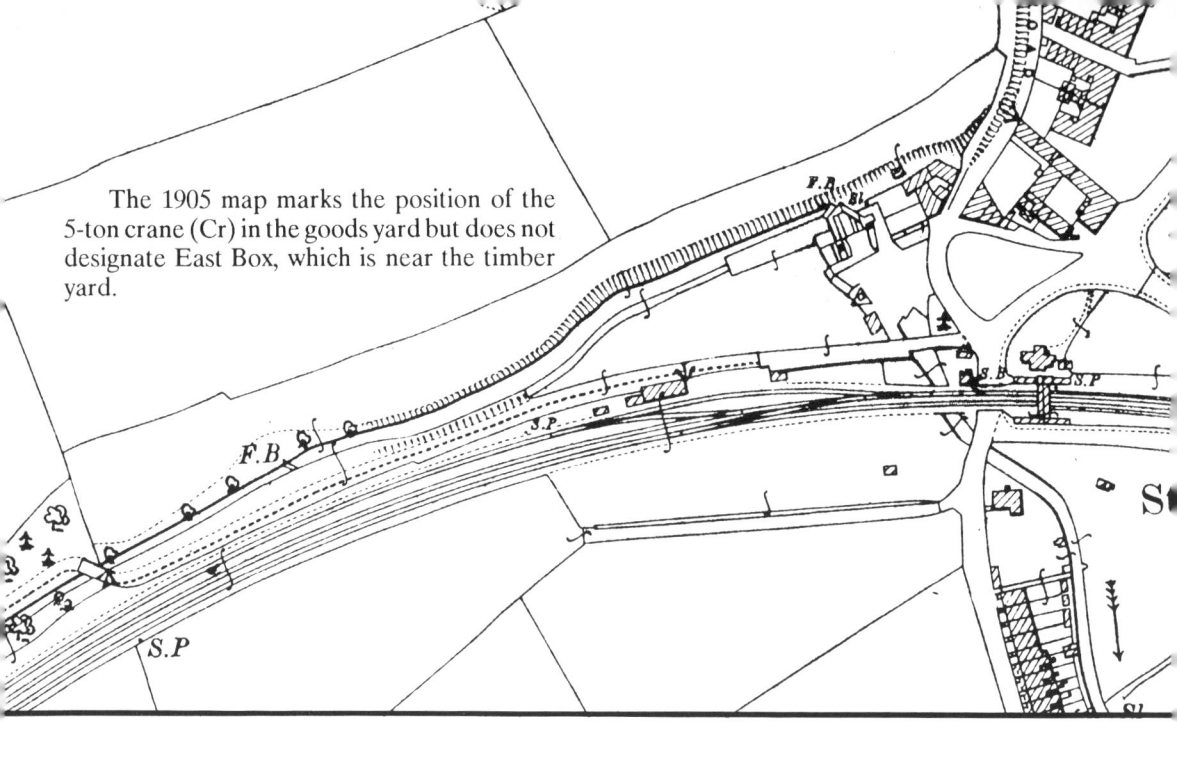

The 1905 map marks the position of the 5-ton crane (Cr) in the goods yard but does not designate East Box, which is near the timber yard.

22. A semi-mobile office was located by one of the early goods buildings when class N 2-6-0 no. 31830 was recorded on 11th August 1954. The lattice signal post was a standard LSWR design. The ex-GWR clerestorey coach was numbered W9029. (H.C.Casserley)

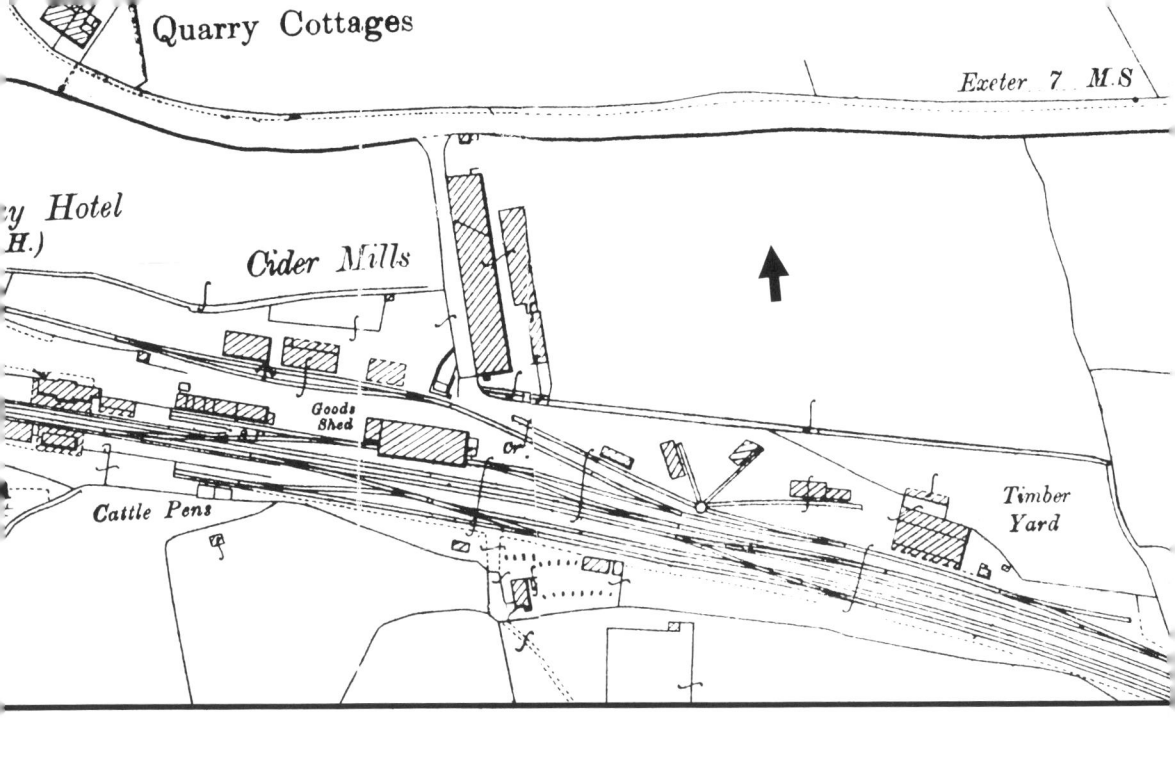

23. Assorted coaches of some antiquity form the 2.45pm Plymouth to Exeter Central on 18th July 1959. Nos. D6302 and D6303 seem to provide an excess of power, but this type usually worked in pairs at that time. (S.C.Nash)

24. The short-lived car carrying service between Okehampton and Surbiton was little photographed but here it is on 30th July 1960, hauled by no. 34056 *Croydon*, a "Battle of Britain" class. The hilly and windy Devon roads were notorious for traffic jams in the summers of the era. The train ran in the summers of 1960-64. (S.C.Nash)

25. The brick-built goods shed was replaced by the structure on the left in the late 1950s but goods traffic ceased on 4th December 1967. Beyond is the cider store and beyond this is the former East Box which was reduced to a ground frame in about 1916 and taken out of use in 1970. A single railcar sufficed for the Exeter - Okehampton service on 26th June 1971. (D.Mitchell)

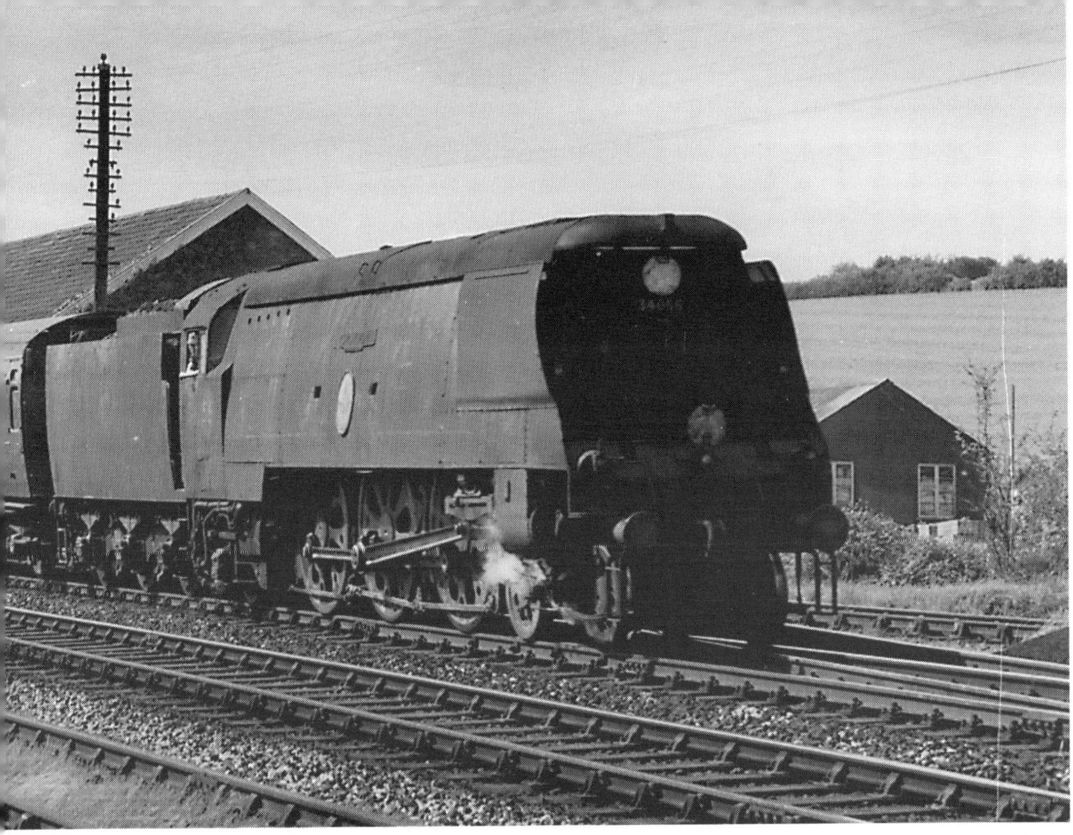

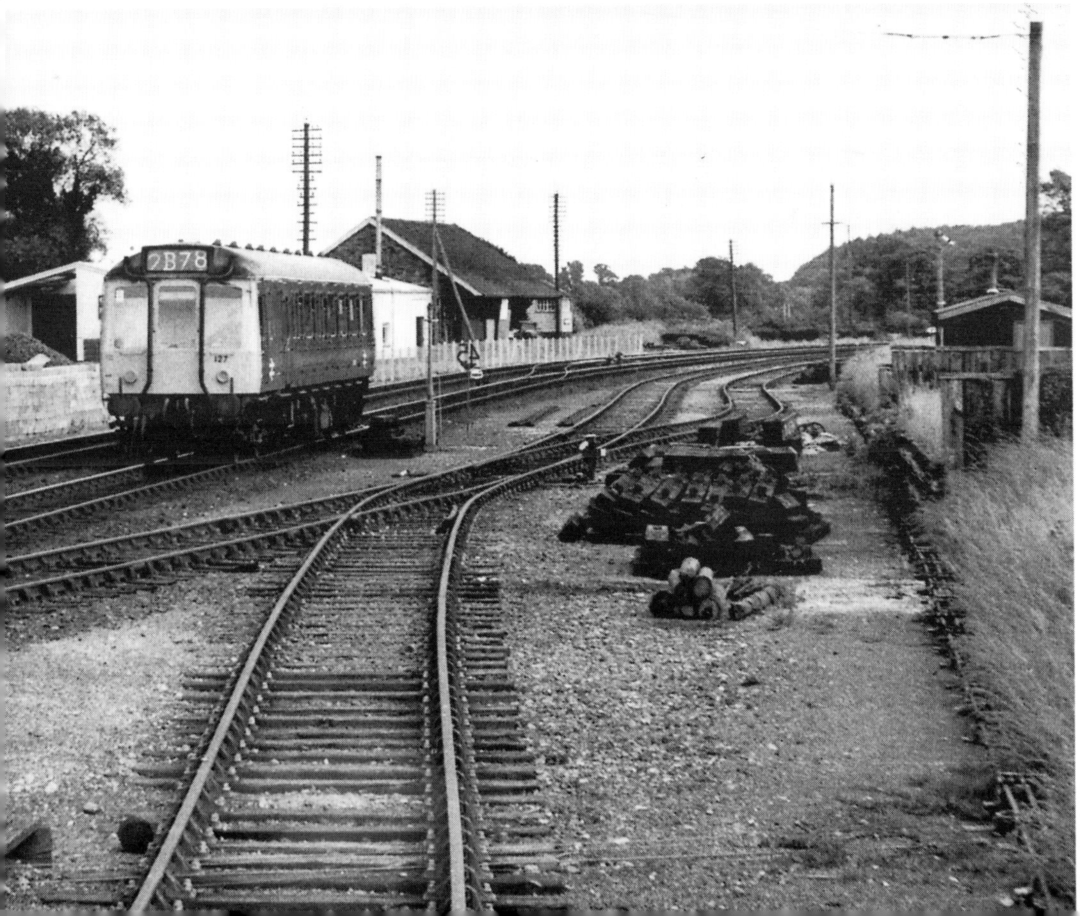
2B78

26. Class 25 no. D7506 creeps through the down platform on 18th July 1972 with empty milk tankers bound for Torrington. The platforms are gas lit while the gates carry oil lamps. (G.Gillham)

```
(663)        SOUTH WESTERN RAILWAY.
         FOR DROVERS OR DEALERS.
                  THIRD CLASS.
No. 99                          Station            187
          PASS  CREDITON              , by      o'clock Train,
from                       to                    , in charge
of                                                 the property
of Mr.                            , of
                                                         
   This Ticket is required to be shown to the attendant by the passenger on taking his seat, and must
              be delivered to the Ticket Collector at the end of the journey.
        This Ticket is issued to, and accepted by the Holder, subject to the conditions on the back.
```

AVAILABLE FOR ONE ONLY.

```
London & South Western Ry.
This Ticket is issued subject to the Regulations
& Conditions stated in the Company's Time
Tables & Bills
EXETER St. DAVID'S to
CREDITON
St. David's            St. David's
Crediton              Crediton
1st CLASS   (S.1)   1st CLASS
Fare 1/1              Fare 1/1
```

Crediton	1928	1936
No. of passenger tickets issued	19788	8724
No. of season tickets issued	101	112
No. of tickets collected	22448	12898
No. of telegrams	5224	3805
Parcels forwarded	5366	3877
Parcels received	10610	16416
Horses forwarded	37	12
Milk forwarded - cans 1928/gallons 1936	1116	8303
Milk received - cans 1928/gallons 1936	-	21
General goods forwarded (tons)	2674	2173
General goods received (tons)	6339	10465
Coal, Coke etc.	6667	6893
Other minerals forwarded	298	330
Other minerals received	8763	4195
Trucks livestock forwarded	409	364
Trucks livestock received	207	40
Lavatory pennies	264	398

27. The former West Box is seen from the footbridge on 13th June 1990 as the driver of no. 33117 passes the token to the signalman. This is the 11.20 Meldon Quarry to Tonbridge stone train. Since 17th October 1971, the double track west hereof has been operated as two single lines. (D.Mitchell)

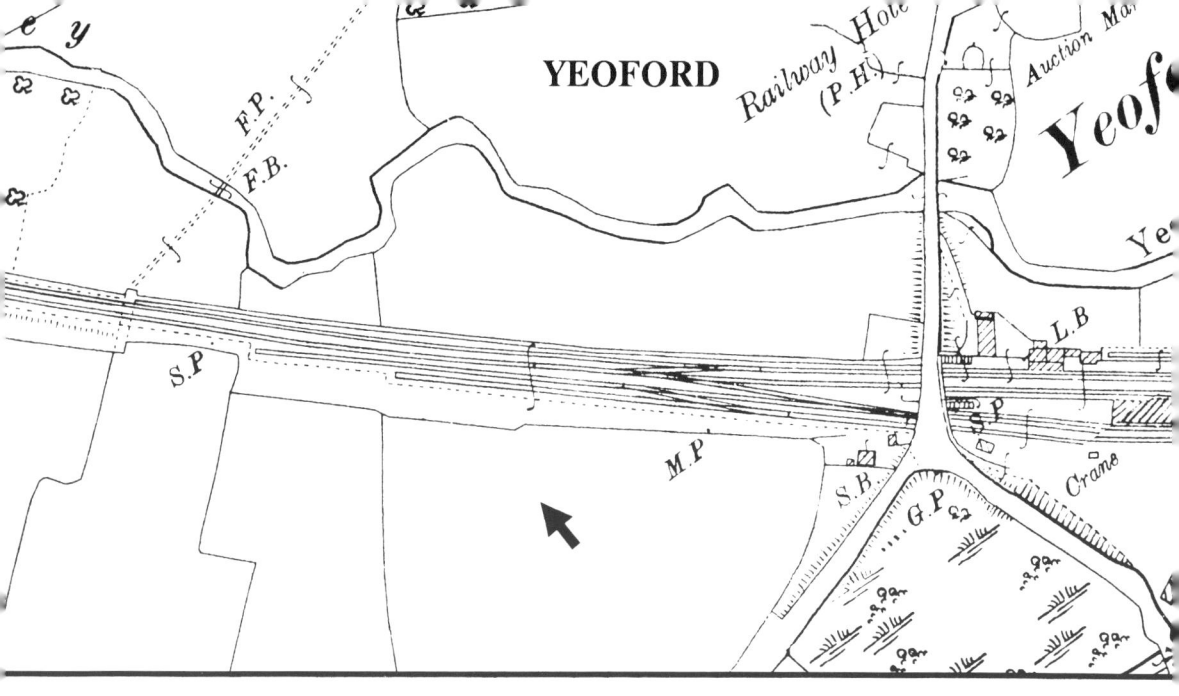

The 1905 survey marks the ground frame S.B. (above the Cattle Pens). In 1933 it was moved to the east of the loop. The River Yeo runs across the upper part of the map. The "Auction Mart" near the Railway Hotel generated a considerable traffic in livestock on the railway.

28. The station became a junction in 1865. Although an island platform, the face on the right was used only for starting down trains, i.e. as a bay platform. Six marshalling sidings are in the distance, these having been increased from three during WWII. In 1942 a connection was added to allow down freight trains direct access to the loop platform; it was not signalled for passenger working. (D.J.W.Brough)

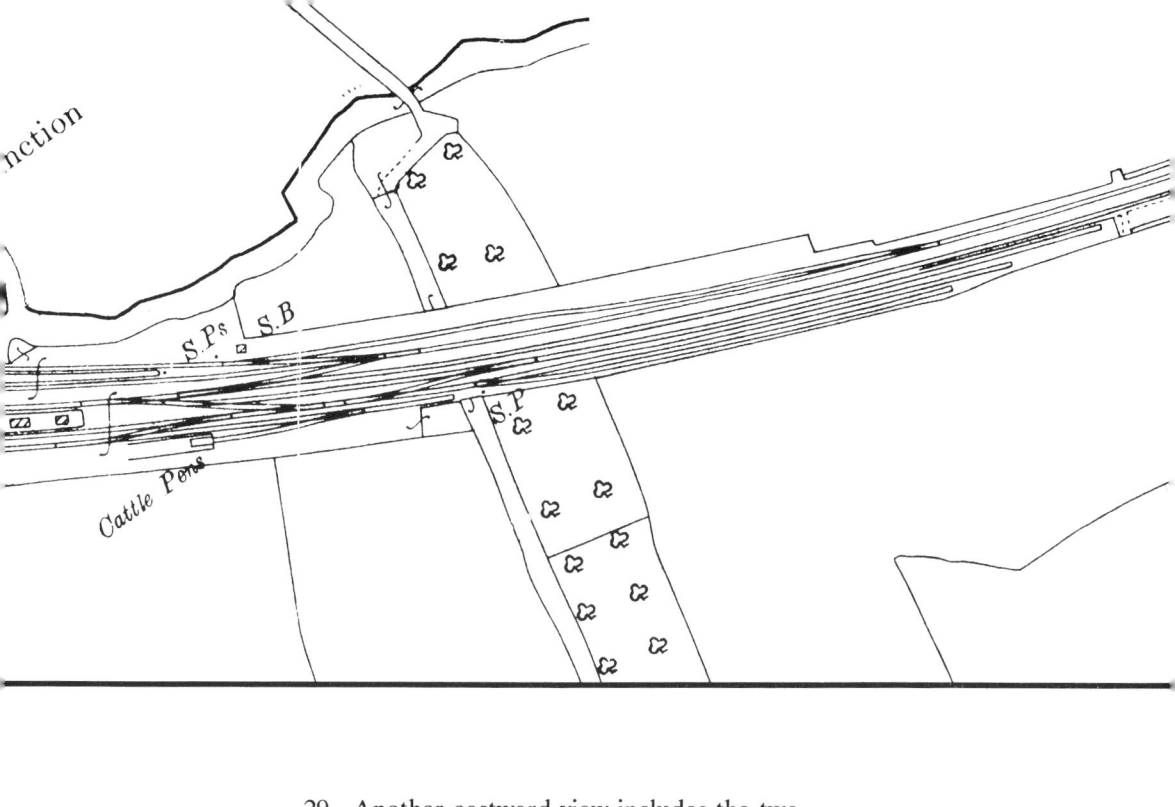

29. Another eastward view includes the two through platforms. There had been much exchange of traffic between North and South Devon here. The steel bridge span had replaced a single brick arch. (Wessex coll.)

Yeoford	1928	1936
No. of passenger tickets issued	12807	7842
No. of season tickets issued	30	20
No. of tickets collected	13262	8640
No. of telegrams	4580	2754
Parcels forwarded	538	360
Parcels received	894	640
Horses forwarded	15	4
Milk forwarded - cans 1928/gallons 1936	2080	15458
Milk received - cans 1928/gallons 1936	-	-
General goods forwarded (tons)	895	477
General goods received (tons)	1127	712
Coal, Coke etc.	262	258
Other minerals forwarded	-	23
Other minerals received	1949	447
Trucks livestock forwarded	118	62
Trucks livestock received	70	11
Lavatory pennies	240	207

30. Class T9 no. 30313 waits with an up freight while the driver holds his tea can and the fireman drinks from a bottle. The footbridge segregated passengers from road traffic. (D.Cullum coll.)

31. Although the water column was well lagged, a brazier was provided nearby to prevent freezing of the essential water. The wire and hook were provided for hoisting Tilley oil lamps. (Wessex coll.)

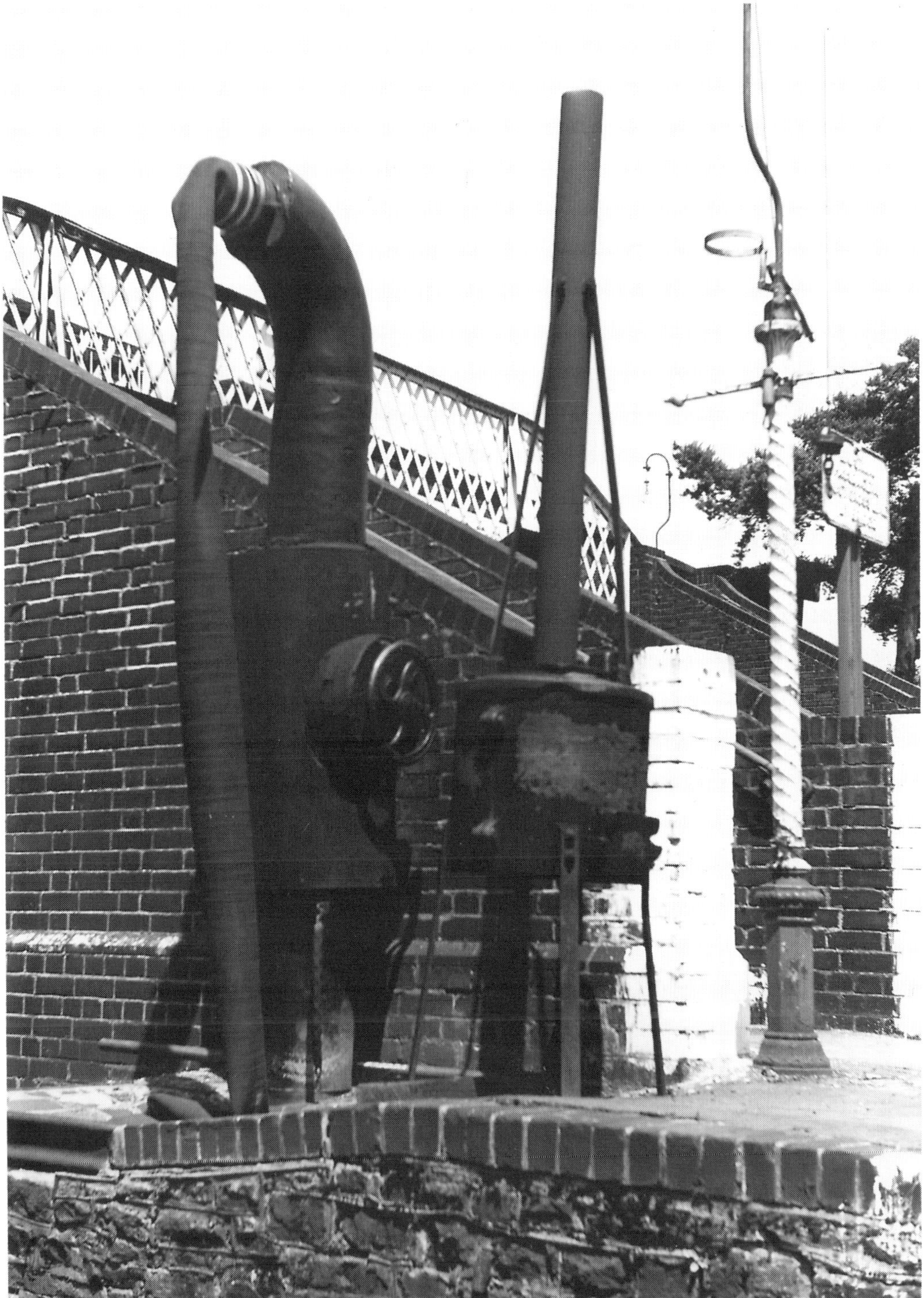

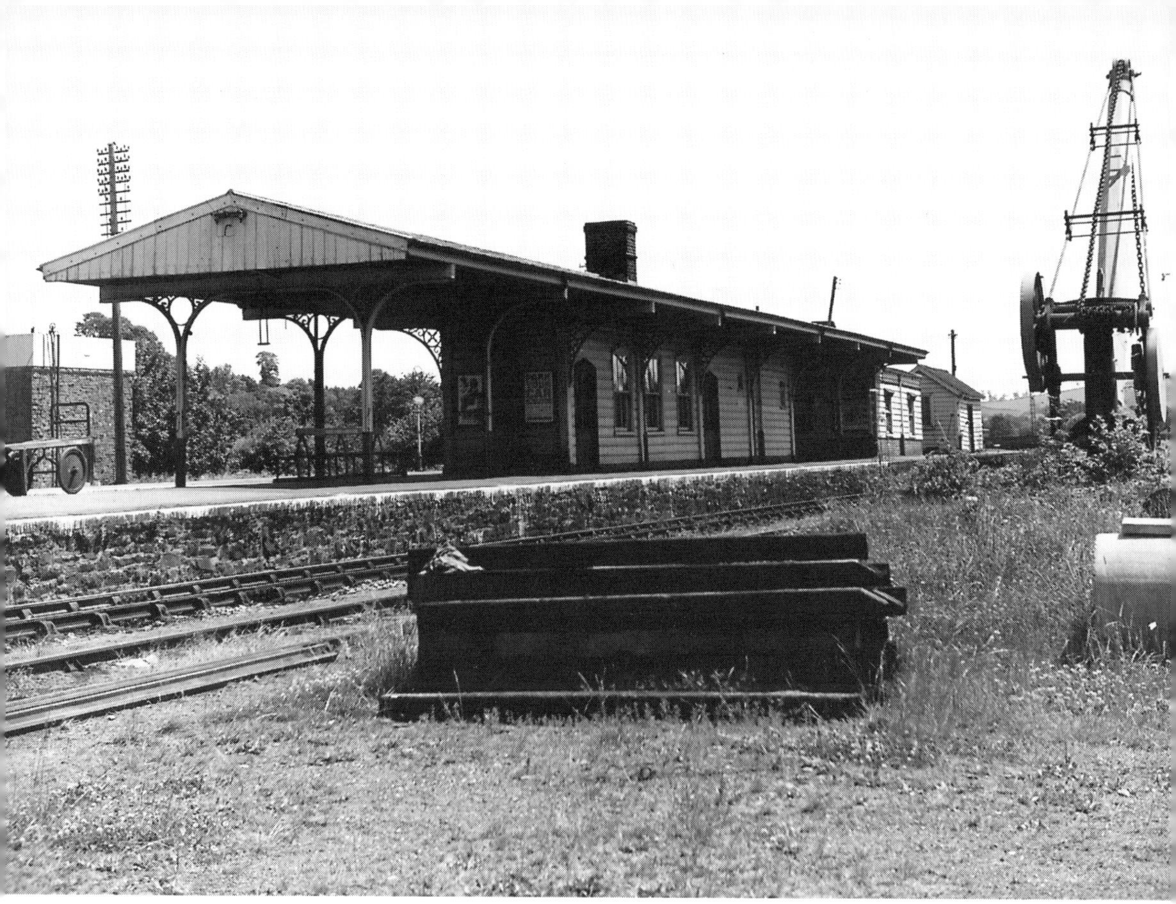

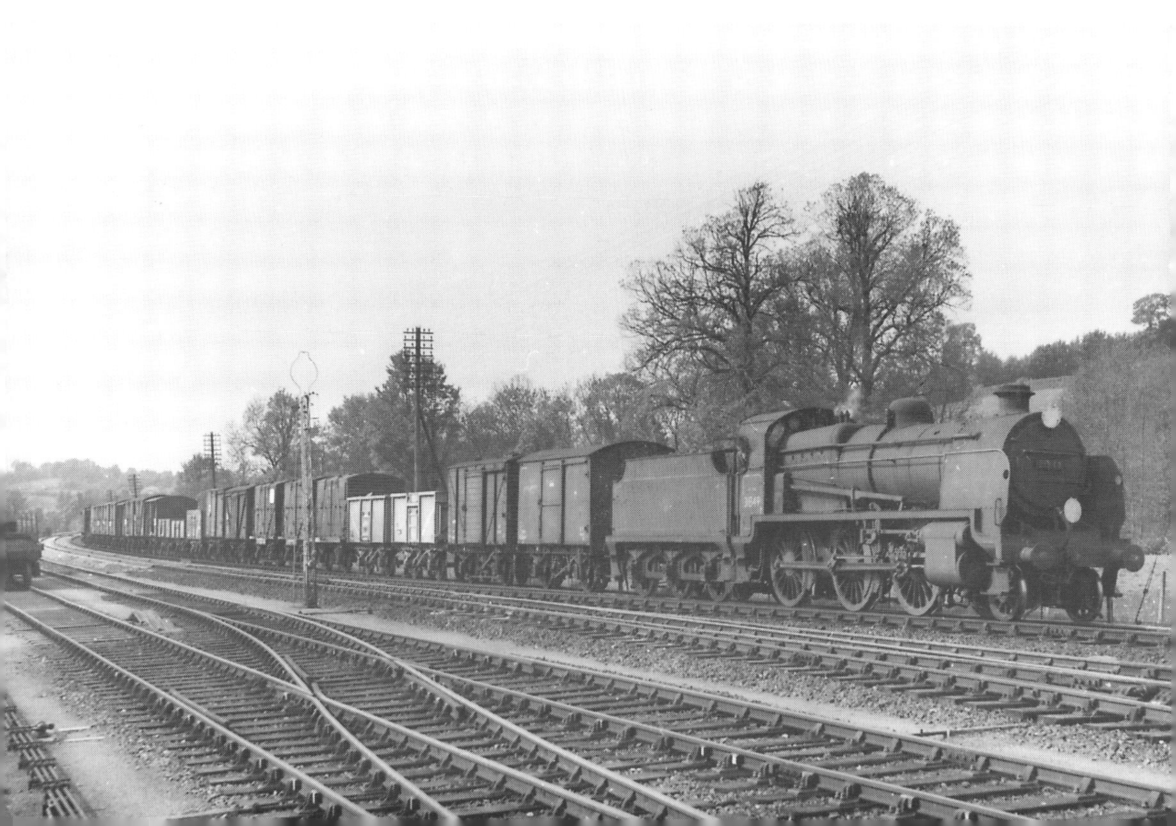

32. The down platform building accommodated a refreshment room for many years, necessary for passengers changing trains at this remote outpost. The 5-ton capacity crane ceased to be used when goods traffic was curtailed on 10th February 1964.
(Wessex coll.)

Other views of the stations from Exeter to Yeoford can be found in our *Exeter to Barnstaple* album.

33. The photographer is standing close to the signal box as N class no. 31849 arrives with freight from the Plymouth line on 7th May 1960. The box closed on 18th August 1968.
(S.C.Nash)

34. Two return journeys between Exeter and Okehampton were operated on four Saturdays in the summer of 1986. The "Dartmoor Rambler" is seen on 16th August, formed of units numbered 142023 and 142019.
(D.Mitchell)

COLEFORD JUNCTION

35. Taken through the dirty windscreen of a DMU forming the 13.35 Exeter to Okehampton, this view shows the junction at Coleford on 3rd April 1969, with the line to Barnstaple going straight ahead. The signal is an ex-LSWR structure but fitted with later pattern arms. The box here was closed on 17th October 1971 when both routes were converted to single track. (G.Gillham)

36. Viewed from the Okehampton line, the 13.26 Exeter Central to Barnstaple speeds past the site of the junction on 28th January 1986. High specification track is provided for the heavy stone trains; see also picture 34. (D.Mitchell)

The 1906 survey includes wagon turntables.

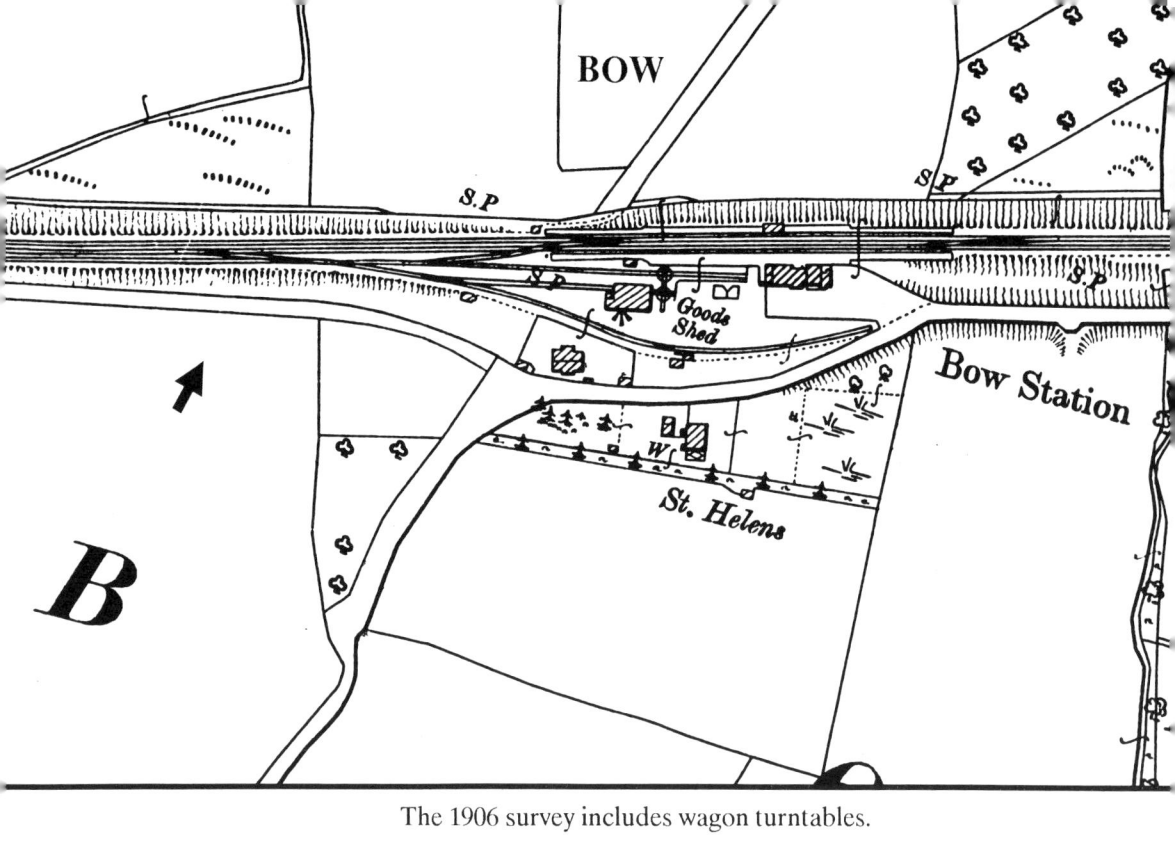

37. The station was situated about one mile south of the village the population of which declined from 944 in 1851 to 608 by 1961. All traffic figures were low, the high 1928 tonnage for minerals probably being due to local road improvement work. (Lens of Sutton)

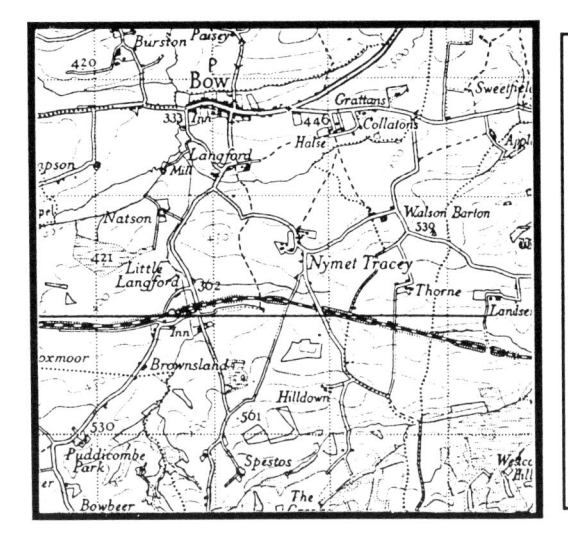

BOW	1928	1936
No. of passenger tickets issued	8600	3723
No. of season tickets issued	14	70
No. of tickets collected	9746	4784
No. of telegrams	637	23
Parcels forwarded	1075	809
Parcels received	1282	1214
Horses forwarded	7	2
Milk forwarded - cans 1928/gallons 1936	-	-
Milk received - cans 1928/gallons 1936	-	-
General goods forwarded (tons)	654	100
General goods received (tons)	1234	623
Coal, Coke etc. received (tons)	729	611
Other minerals forwarded (tons)	28	~~601~~
Other minerals received (tons)	1850	601
Trucks livestock forwarded	166	129
Trucks livestock received	43	18
Lavatory pennies	156	162

38. This and the next two pictures were taken on 3rd August 1955. This one includes the goods shed and loading gauge; the yard closed on 1st May 1961. (D.Cullum)

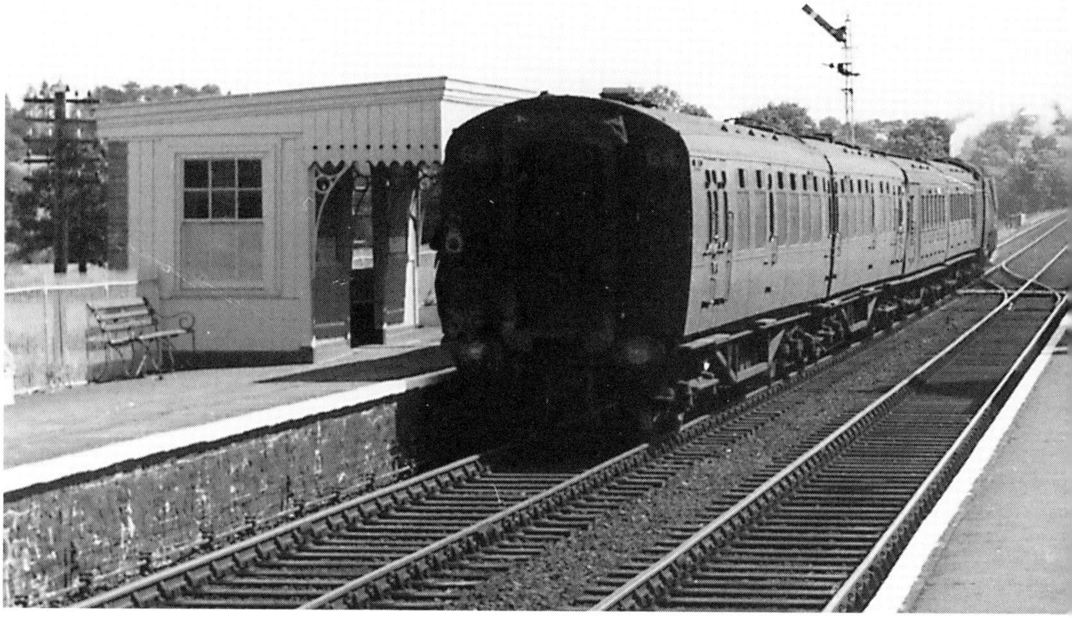

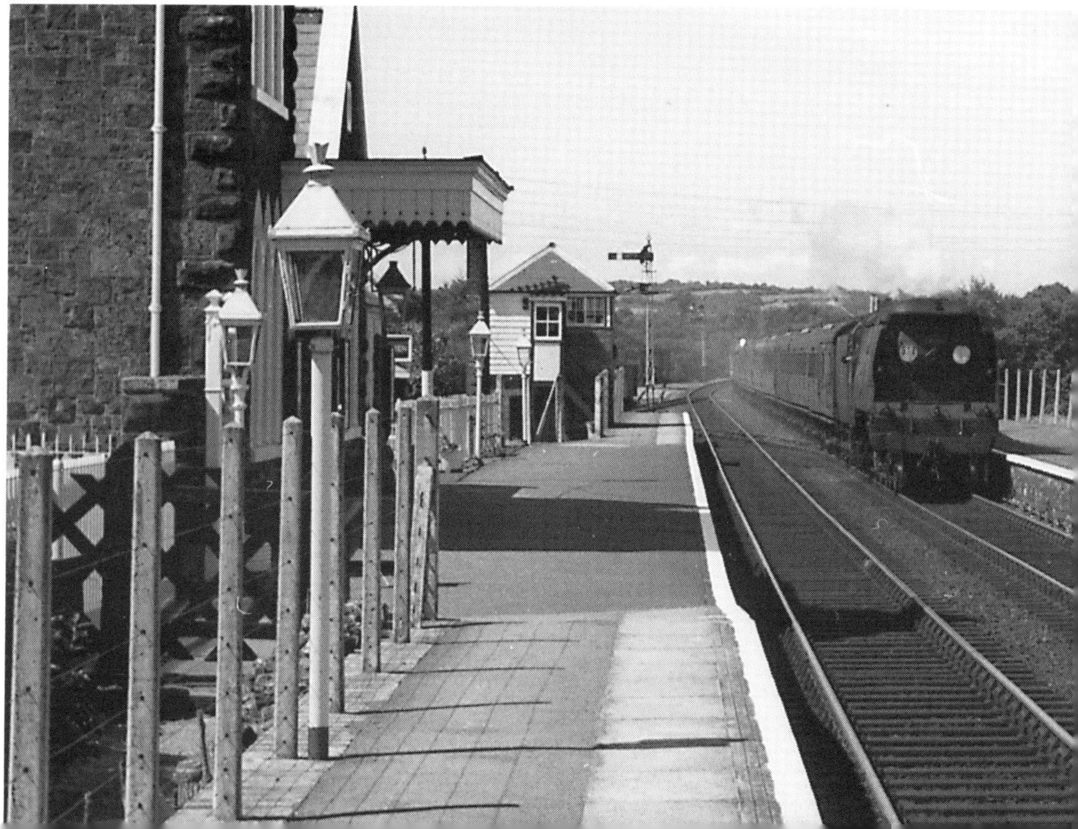

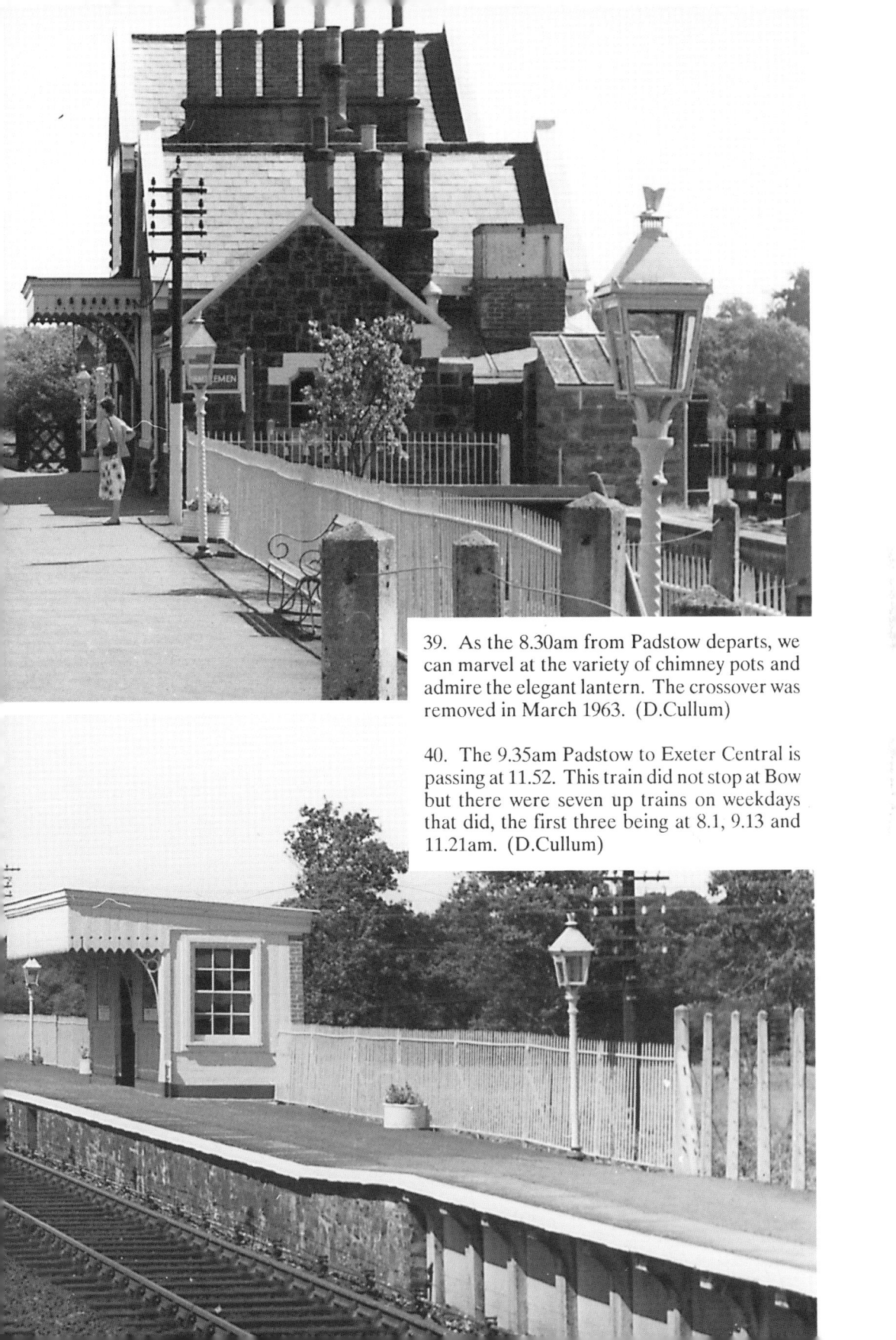

39. As the 8.30am from Padstow departs, we can marvel at the variety of chimney pots and admire the elegant lantern. The crossover was removed in March 1963. (D.Cullum)

40. The 9.35am Padstow to Exeter Central is passing at 11.52. This train did not stop at Bow but there were seven up trains on weekdays that did, the first three being at 8.1, 9.13 and 11.21am. (D.Cullum)

41. Between the goods shed and the signal box was the cattle dock siding. There were three sidings in total. The box was closed on 21st January 1964. (Wessex coll.)

42. Evidence of decay was to be found in March 1982 by which time only stone trains passed regularly on the one remaining track. This was a private residence in 1995. (D.Mitchell)

NORTH TAWTON

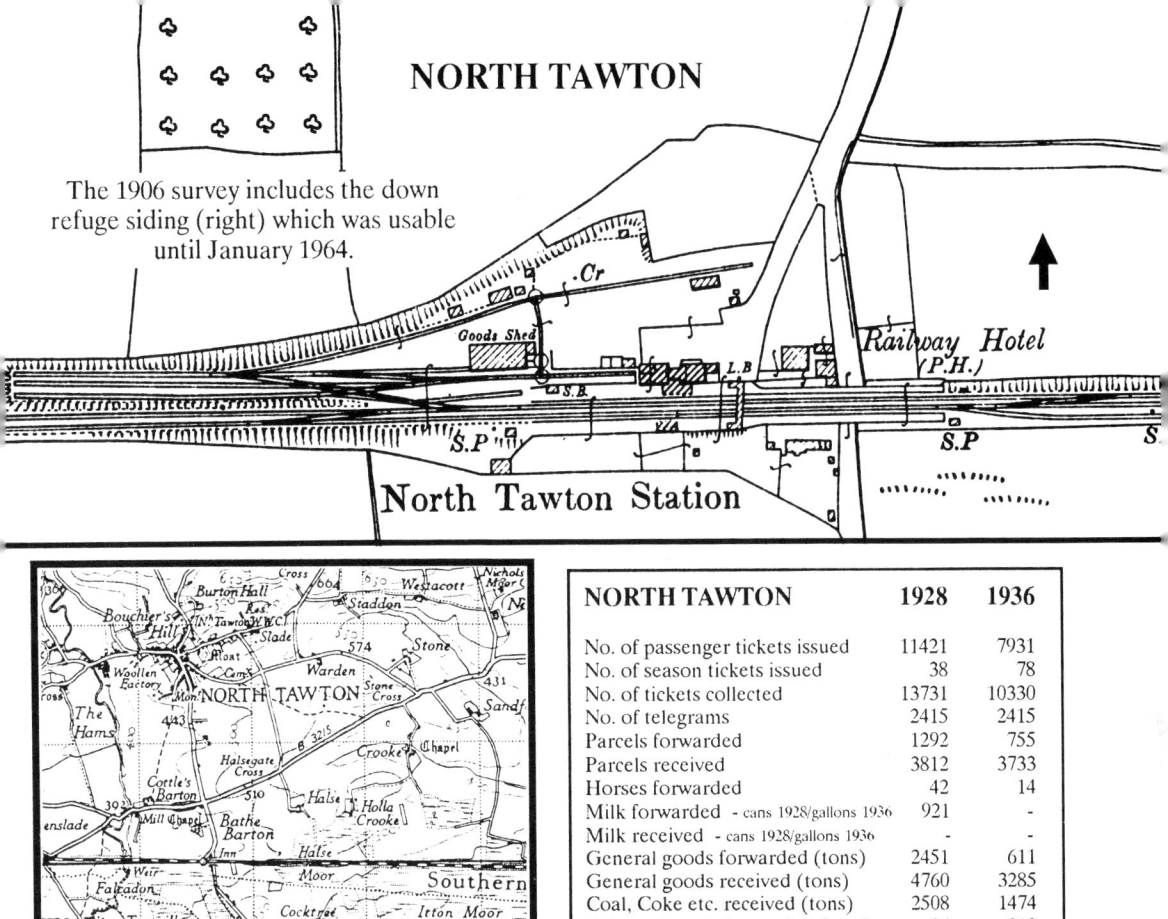

The 1906 survey includes the down refuge siding (right) which was usable until January 1964.

North Tawton Station

NORTH TAWTON	1928	1936
No. of passenger tickets issued	11421	7931
No. of season tickets issued	38	78
No. of tickets collected	13731	10330
No. of telegrams	2415	2415
Parcels forwarded	1292	755
Parcels received	3812	3733
Horses forwarded	42	14
Milk forwarded - cans 1928/gallons 1936	921	-
Milk received - cans 1928/gallons 1936	-	-
General goods forwarded (tons)	2451	611
General goods received (tons)	4760	3285
Coal, Coke etc. received (tons)	2508	1474
Other minerals forwarded (tons)	26	210
Other minerals received (tons)	1646	2039
Trucks livestock forwarded	142	217
Trucks livestock received	51	33
Lavatory pennies	552	223

43. A covered footbridge is unexpected at a minor station. It was over one mile south of the village which dropped from 1500 to 1000 residents in the first six decades of the twentieth century. Note the tapered timber signal post. (Lens of Sutton)

44. Apart from the loss of the footbridge roof, the station was still intact when photographed in August 1955. The crossover at the far end of the platforms was in use until 1967. The footbridge was re-erected at the Mid-Hants Railway's Ropley station in 1986. (D.Cullum)

45. A January 1965 photograph includes the box which closed on 24th September 1967 and the goods yard which had ceased to handle traffic on 7th September 1964. (C.L.Caddy)

46. Unlike its neighbours, this station was wired for electric lighting. The down platform shelter was photographed in 1967 and removed in 1994 for reuse on the Mid-Hants Railway. (Wessex coll.)

47. The north elevation was recorded in 1967, along with British Railway's Railfreight van then conveying parcel traffic. (Wessex coll.)

48. No. 45022 is seen from the footbridge on 22nd March 1982 as it conveys stone from Meldon Quarry to Bristol. It is on a short rising gradient of 1 in 80 on an otherwise long descent. (D.Mitchell)

49. A 1995 photograph reveals that most of the bold architectural features have been retained but that the platform has vanished from view as track level has risen. (D.Dornom)

The line to Okehampton is on the left of this 1906 map.

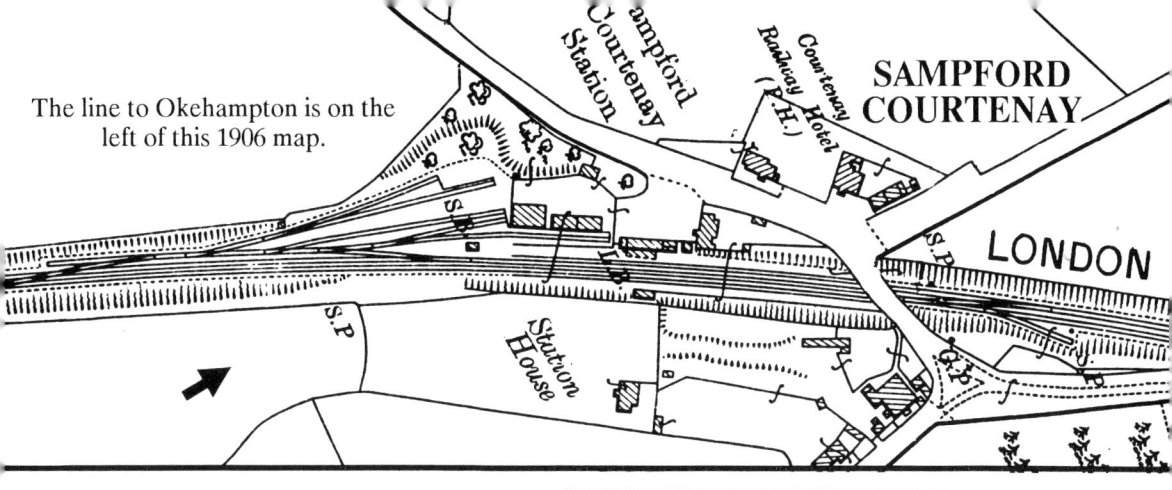

SAMPFORD COURTENAY

LONDON

SAMPFORD COURTENAY 1928		1936
No. of passenger tickets issued	2985	2755
No. of season tickets issued	14	6
No. of tickets collected	3258	3152
No. of telegrams	707	494
Parcels forwarded	220	100
Parcels received	504	332
Horses forwarded	5	5
Milk forwarded - cans 1928/gallons 1936	16	4115
Milk received - cans 1928/gallons 1936	-	11
General goods forwarded (tons)	707	420
General goods received (tons)	1103	1288
Coal, Coke etc. received (tons)	91	114
Other minerals forwarded (tons)	26	-
Other minerals received (tons)	580	457
Trucks livestock forwarded	40	36
Trucks livestock received	205	14
Lavatory pennies	84	60

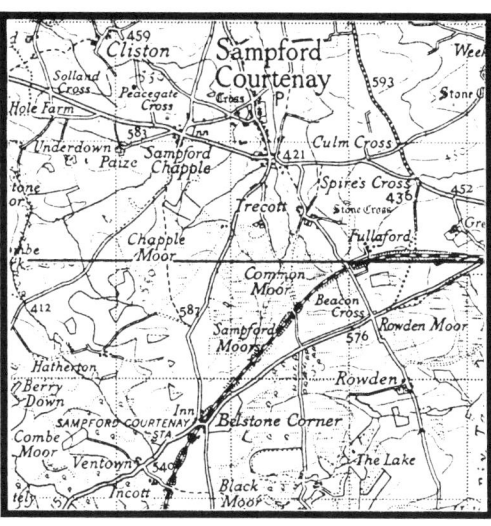

50. Opened as a terminus known as "Okehampton Road", the station was renamed "Belstone Corner" when trains commenced running to Okehampton on 3rd October 1871. It became "Sampford Courtenay" on 1st January 1872, the village of about 700 souls being more than one mile to the north.
(Unknown)

51. No. 34054 *Lord Beaverbrook* speeds through on 3rd October 1964 with the 12.20 Plymouth to Exeter St. Davids. Dieselisation of the route took place on 7th September 1964 so here is a case of steam deputising for a failed diesel. On the right is the grass covered goods yard which had closed on 3rd April 1961. (C.L.Caddy)

52. The station was officially a halt from 12th September 1965 until 5th May 1969, although trains continued to call until 1972. This and the next photograph date from 1967. (Wessex coll.)

53. The size of the goods shed reflected the importance of this traffic in the early years of the line. There was a two-ton crane. The LSWR established an abattoir in the yard but this came under the control of the Ministry of Food in WWI and was leased out in about 1920. The fifth siding was removed in 1930. (Wessex coll.)

54. The disused up side building was still standing unloved in 1982. It was subsequently converted to a dwelling. (D.Mitchell)

EAST OF OKEHAMPTON

55. The 11.47am Exeter Central to Plymouth sweeps round a 30-chain curve as it climbs at 1 in 77 having just crossed the 80yd-long Fatherford Viaduct, visible above the middle coach. The locomotive on 30th May 1959 was no. 34074 *46 Squadron*. The foreground is now part of the A30(T) which forms a bypass to Okehampton. (S.C.Nash)

OKEHAMPTON

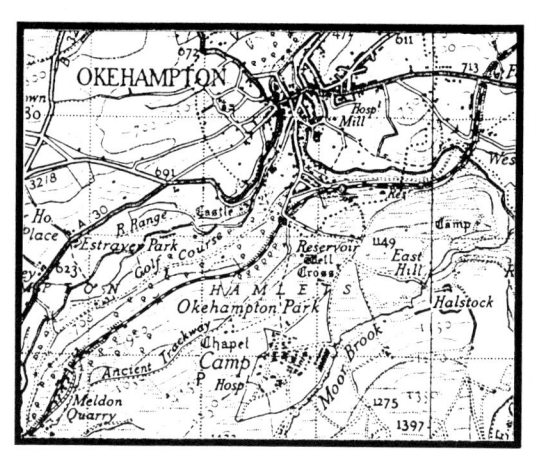

OKEHAMPTON	1928	1936
No. of passenger tickets issued	42537	28599
No. of season tickets issued	58	281
No. of tickets collected	39806	43317
No. of telegrams	20580	12627
Parcels forwarded	9770	5274
Parcels received	19743	23673
Horses forwarded	1898	904
Milk forwarded - cans 1928/gallons 1936	222	8775
Milk received - cans 1928/gallons 1936	-	752
General goods forwarded (tons)	2191	1263
General goods received (tons)	12179	13026
Coal, Coke etc. received (tons)	6976	5909
Other minerals forwarded (tons)	5128	342
Other minerals received (tons)	5820	2585
Trucks livestock forwarded	297	233
Trucks livestock received	127	51
Lavatory pennies	11	4491

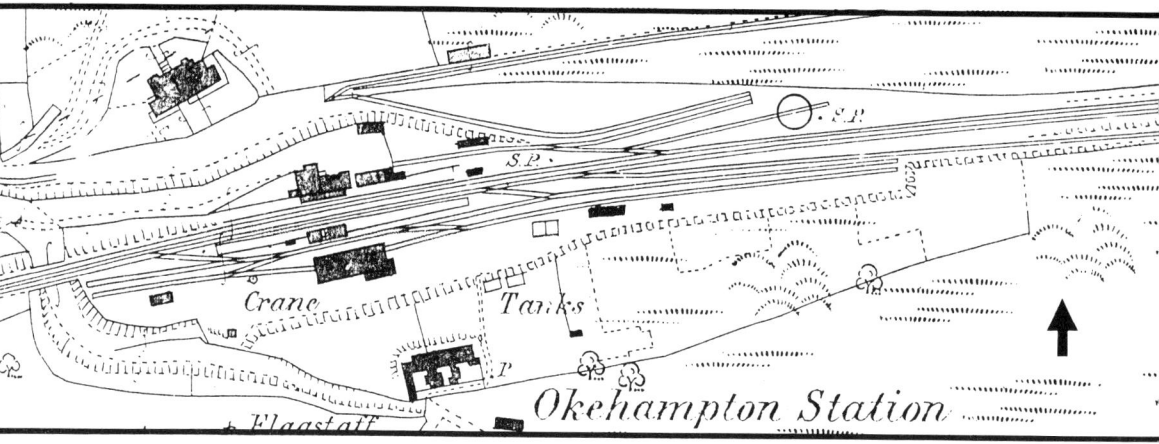

The first edition of 1885 has the line from Exeter on the right. At the top is part of the Fatherford Tramway which ran to a quarry near Belstone.

56. The up platform was protected by a glazed wind shield (left) and a canopy, the valence of which was painted salmon pink and brown on alternate boards. There was also a refreshment room on the down platform. (Unknown)

57. West of the station were two long platforms for use by military traffic to and from the training areas on Dartmoor. This photograph dates from 1913. The car carrying train shown in picture no. 24 would have started its journey here. The sidings were taken out of use in 1982. (Lens of Sutton)

58. An up train passes under the fully glazed footbridge with a train of attractive pink and brown coaches. The signal box on the left was in use until 1935. (Lens of Sutton)

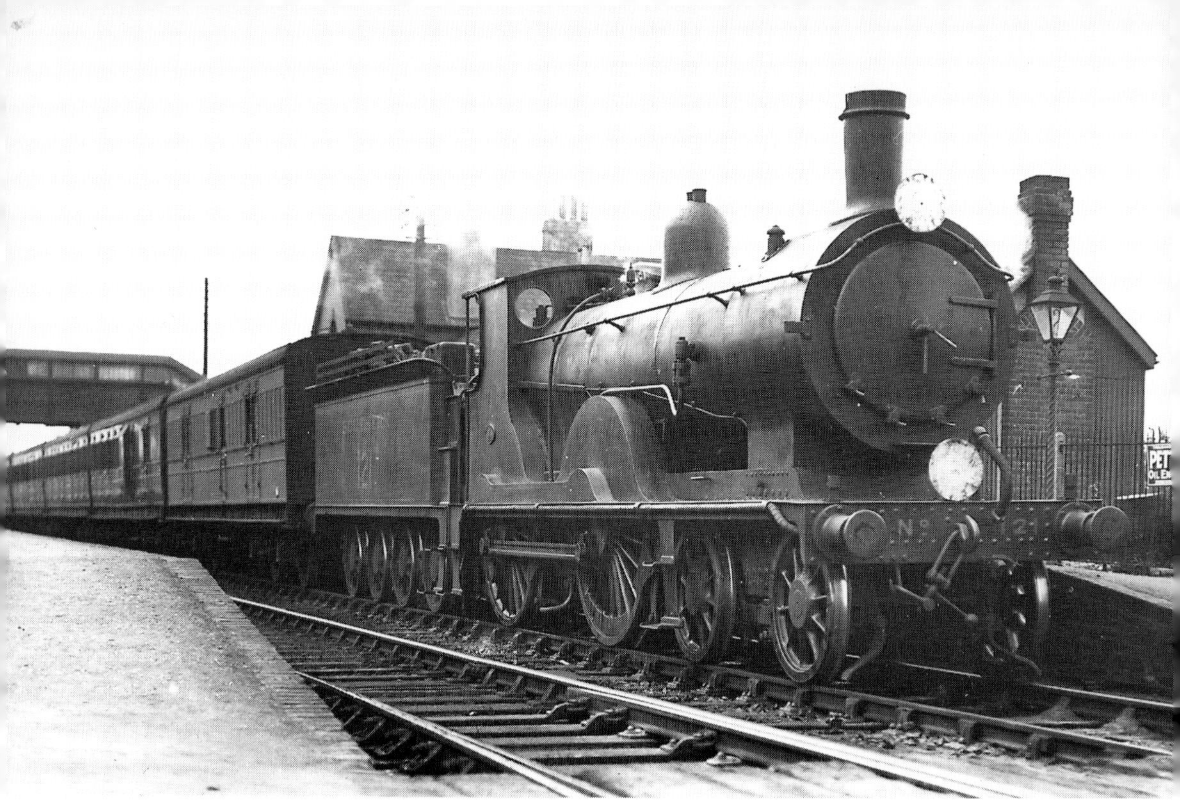
Nº
121

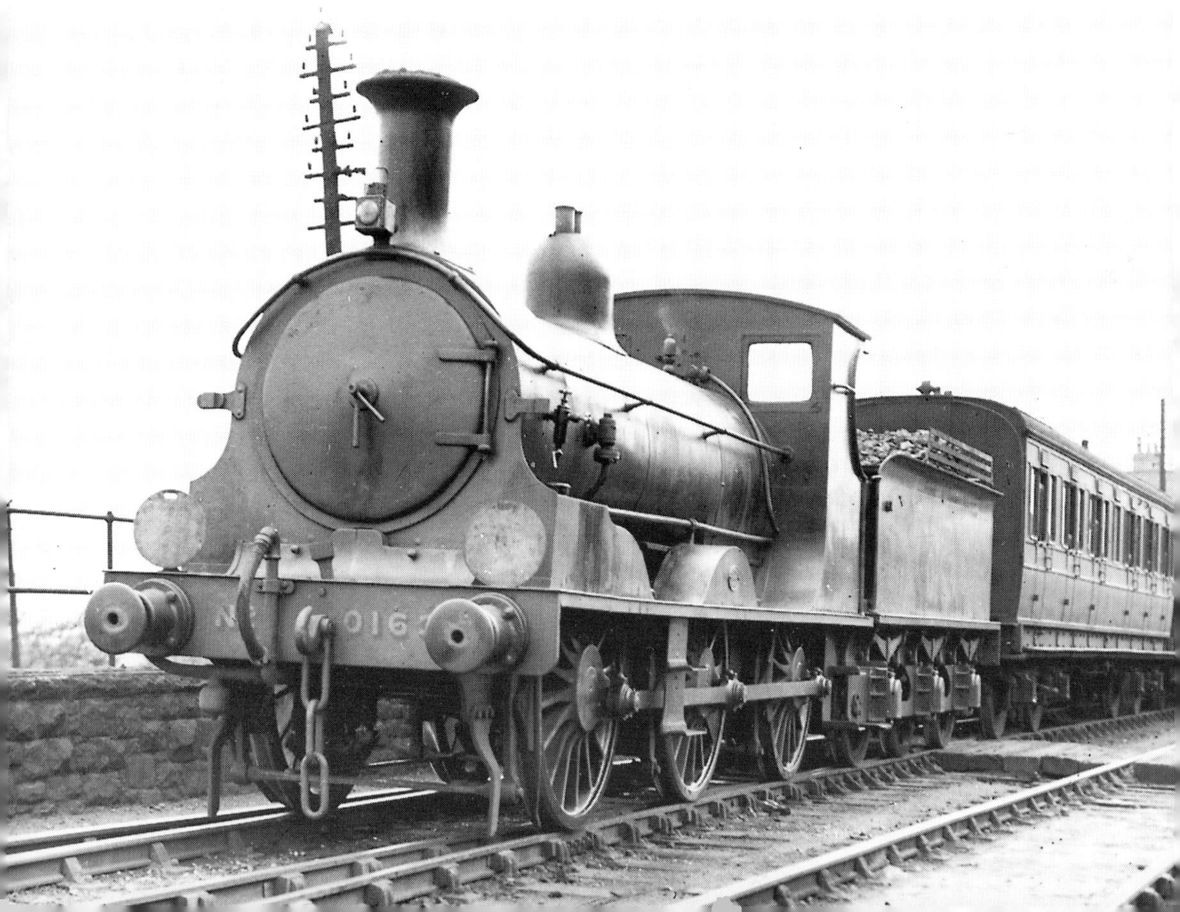
Nº
016

59. The 8.30am Plymouth Friary to Exeter Central was hauled by class T9 no. 121 on 3rd August 1928. It stopped at all stations except one. By that time, the trains had been repainted green. Many down trains were divided here, the Plymouth portion usually leaving first. (H.C.Casserley)

60. Pictured on the same day is no. 0163, an 0395 class built in 1883 by Neilson, which survived until 1956. The second vehicle is a horse box, a vehicle type which could often be found running in passenger trains. (H.C.Casserley)

61. A new 70ft turntable and coaling stage at the east end of the up platform were ready for use on 12th October 1947. The previous 50ft turntable had been close to the engine shed. (Wessex coll.)

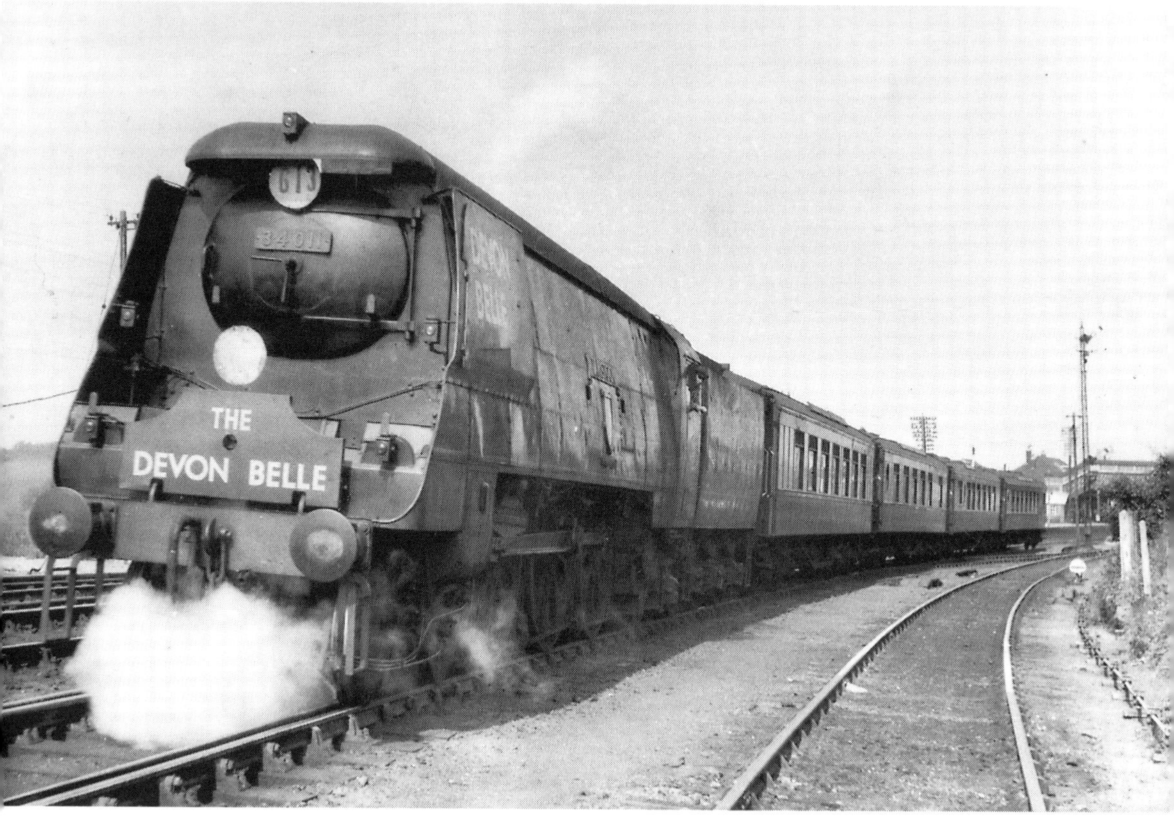
THE
DEVON BELLE
DEVON
BELLE

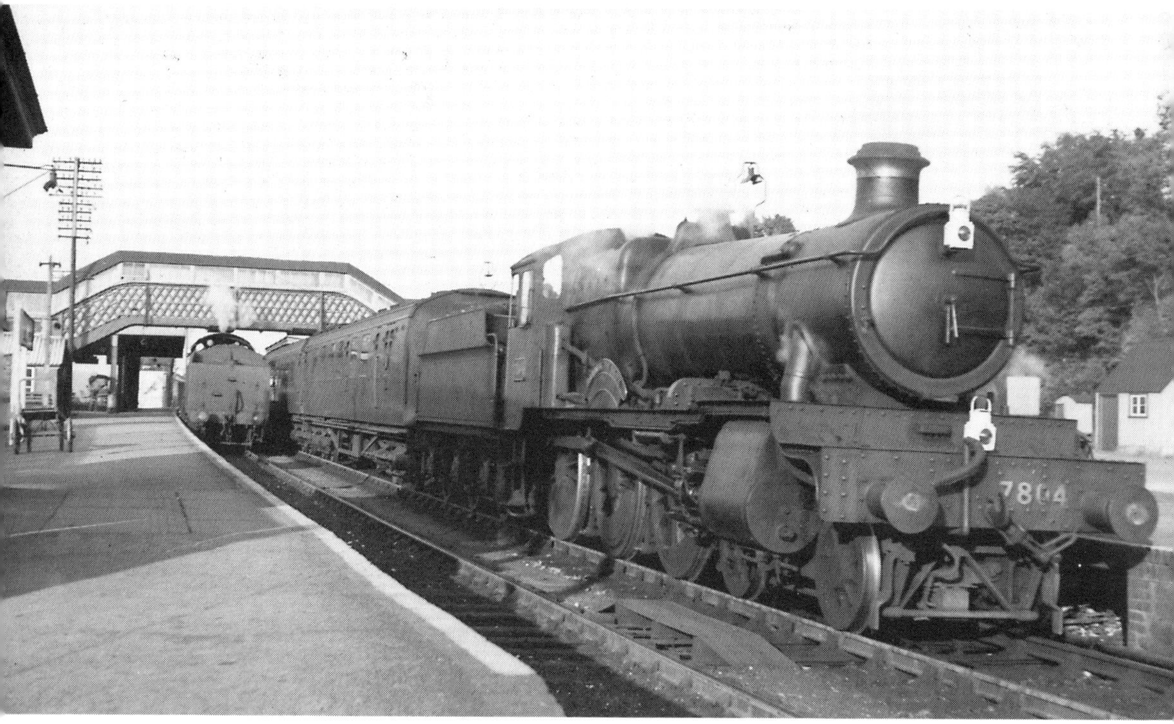
7804

62. The all-Pullman "Devon Belle" (Plymouth portion) was recorded on 16th June 1949. No. 34011 *Tavistock* carries the train name above its buffer beam and on its smoke deflectors. The headshunt on the right was removed in 1966. (S.C.Nash)

> **Other pictures of this station and Meldon Quarry can be seen in the companion album,** *Branch Line to Bude.*

64. The shed was constructed in 1920 after its timber-built predecessor had been destroyed by fire. No. 34035 *Shaftesbury* stands on the previous turntable site on 30th May 1959. (S.C.Nash)

63. Western Region no. 7804 *Baydon Manor* was working the Plymouth portion of the 2.50pm from Waterloo on 20th June 1949. It became a common practice for locomotive crews to maintain route knowledge of both lines between Exeter and Plymouth in case of diversion. (S.C.Nash)

65. Class N 2-6-0 no. 31831 was receiving little shelter on 6th December 1959. The shed was built with only three roof ventilators (two more were added later) but by then the subject was rather academic. It was repaired later. (M.E.J.Dart)

66. The first quarter of 1963 brought the coldest weather in living memory, the temperature being below freezing point almost continuously for three months. No. 34056 *Croydon* arrives with a train from Waterloo on 8th February 1963. (R.E.Ruffell)

67. Frequent heavy snowfalls demanded regular use of snowploughs. Q class no. 30530 arrived on 8th February 1963 to replace a locomotive that had failed during clearance work. The missing gradient post arm showed "L" for Level. The 1 in 77 climb continued for two miles west of the station. (R.E.Ruffell)

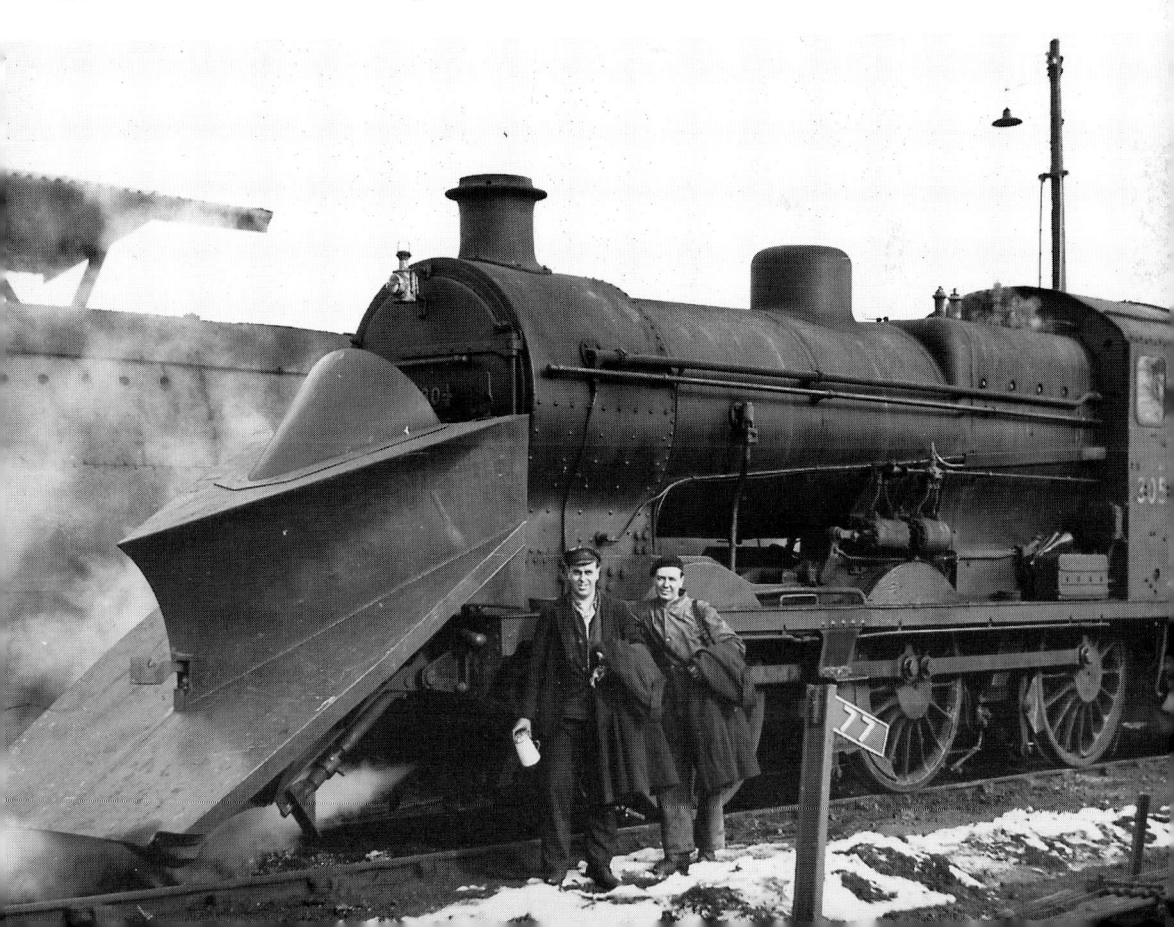

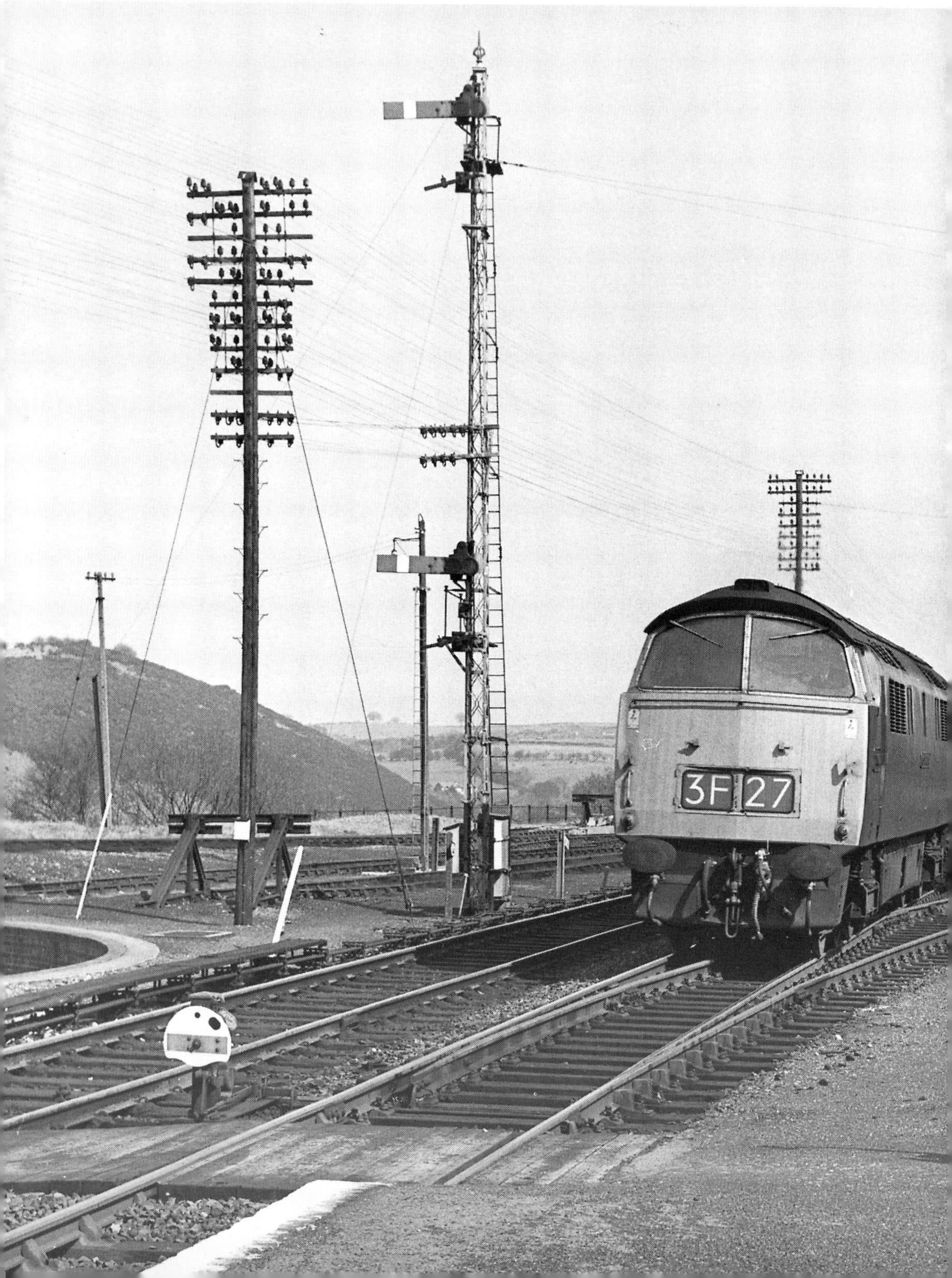
3F27

68. With an altitude of about 750 ft above sea level, the station was prone to severe weather. A single railcar from Exeter terminates at platform 2 on 28th December 1968, while a connecting coach for Bude waits in the car park. Previously the connection would have been standing at platform 1. (E.Wilmshurst)

69. No. D1067 *Western Druid* brings its train of empty ballast wagons to the top of the incline on 3rd April 1969. The signalling was functional until the box closed on 10th July 1972. A crane of 7½ ton capacity had been available in the goods yard. (G.Gillham)

70. The up side buildings had been completely rebuilt in 1932 and are seen here soon after the withdrawal of passenger service on 5th June 1972. The refreshment counter was recovered for reuse at Alresford on the Mid-Hants Railway. (Wessex coll.)

71. A number of special trains for railway enthusiasts have passed through. On 6th May 1989, two 4TC sets were recorded. They were being propelled back from Meldon Quarry by nos. 33106 and 33119. In addition to the trains mentioned in caption 34, there had been some for Christmas shopping and others in connection with a coach tour of closed stations. (S.C.Nash)

72. No. D6508 (alias 33008) *Eastleigh* runs east on 30th April 1993. The line from Meldon Quarry had been singled on 22nd March 1970 and that to Crediton on 17th October 1971. A loop had been retained round the down platform. The signal box (near the rear of the train) had a short life as an office following closure. (D.Mitchell)

73. Goods traffic had ceased in 1979 but several sidings were retained, possibly for potential military use. This February 1994 picture includes the unusual concrete canopy brackets which had been added to the old building seen on the left of picture 58. The line became the property of ECC Quarries Ltd in the following month. (V.Mitchell)

MELDON QUARRY

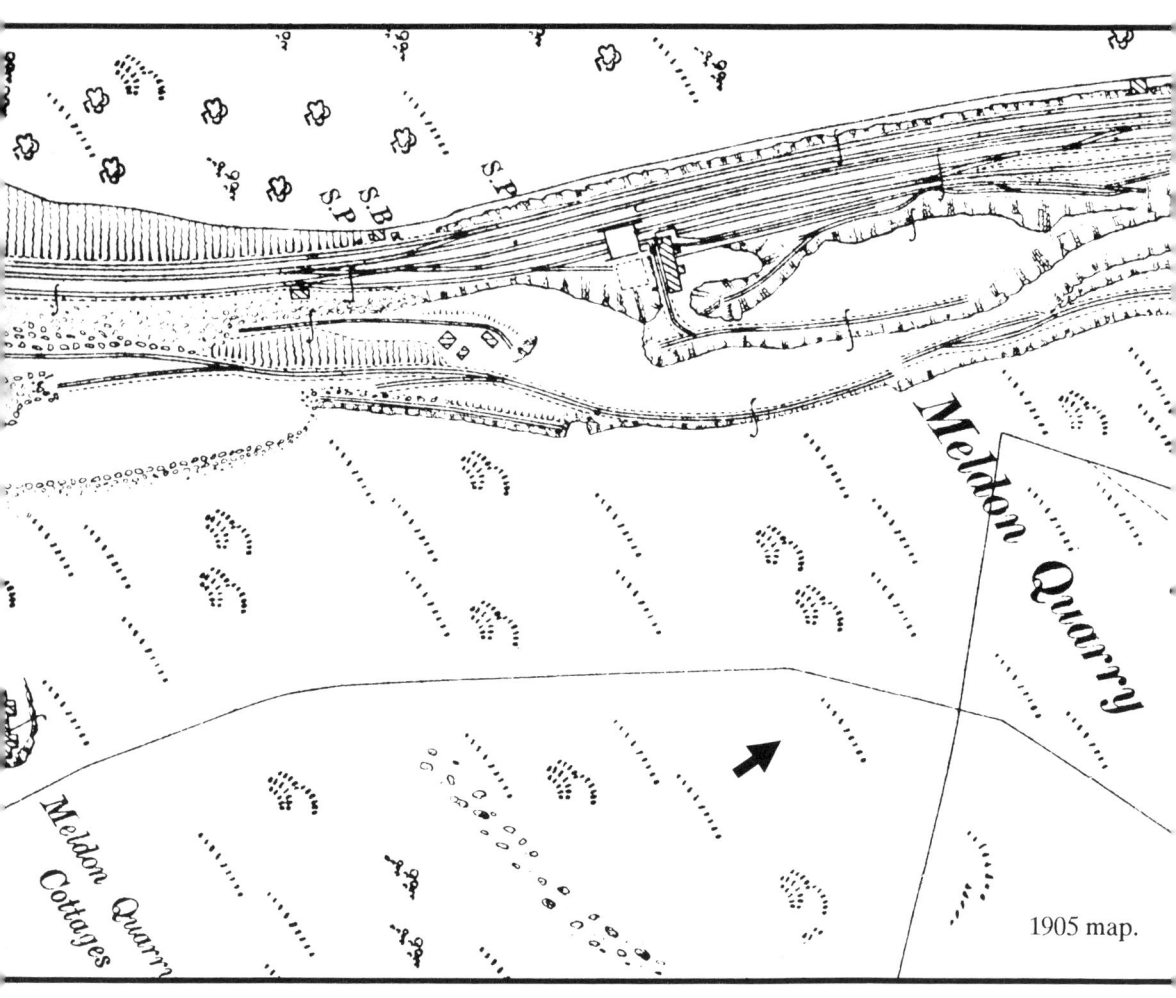

1905 map.

The LSWR established a small quarry for local supplies of track ballast in 1874 and expanded it from 1897 to meet all its requirements, over 100,000 tons being produced annually for many of the early years.

Meldon Quarry.—Blasting operations are frequently carried out at Meldon Quarry, and Drivers must keep a good look-out and be prepared to stop in response to any hand signals that may be exhibited.

Meldon Junction refuge siding.—Whenever wagons are detached from up goods trains at Meldon Junction siding, they must be placed well back in the siding and coupled on to any wagons which may be standing there, and care taken to see that sufficient brakes are pinned down and sprags used to prevent the wagons running away.

74. The down platform of the staff halt is visible as class 460 no. 526 of 1886 waits on 14th July 1924, discharging no steam whatsoever. It is working the 1.5pm Okehampton to Launceston train and was withdrawn in 1928. (H.C.Casserley)

75. Initially horses undertook the shunting but from 1927 this Manning Wardle 0-4-0ST was helping with the work. It had been built in 1881 for the SER to shunt at Folkestone Harbour. It was at Meldon until 1938, numbered 225S. The quarry also supplied aggregates to the SR's concrete works at Exmouth Junction. (H.C.Casserley coll.)

76. The quarry was expanding but the engine shed was collapsing by the time that this photograph was taken on 19th June 1949. By that date the output was over 300,000 tons per annum and the shunting was undertaken by class O2 0-4-4T no. 30232. (S.C.Nash)

77. Snapped from a passing train on 3rd October 1959 is the grading and loading plant, together with the replacement engine shed. It contains class G6 0-6-0T no. DS 3152 (formerly no. 30272) which was on duty here from 1949 until 1960. Another G6 (DS682 formerly no. 30238) worked here until December 1962. (M.E.J.Dart)

78. Class T9 no. 30726 leaves the quarry at 5.10pm on 4th June 1959 bound for Okehampton with the workmen's coach and loaded hoppers. The bridge was built in about 1930 to carry a siding to a dump site on lower ground. (S.C.Nash)

79. Viewed from the bridge on 9th May 1961 is the 1900 reservoir which provided water for ballast washing and also supplied Okehampton station. Ex-GWR class 4300 2-6-0 no. 7316 is working hard with a Plymouth-bound freight. (S.C.Nash)

80. No. DS234 arrived here in December 1962 and was photographed by the small shunt signal on 22nd October 1965. Built in the USA in 1942, it was purchased by the SR in 1947 and became BR no. 30062. Class 08 diesel shunters were introduced in 1966. The signal box closed on 22nd March 1970. (S.C.Nash)

81. Pathfinder Tours "Taw & Tor Tourer" waits on the former up main line on 5th May 1990. This was by then designated the arrival siding. No. 50020 waits to depart. No shunting locomotives were in use then as block trains were universal on the route. (D.Mitchell)

82. Access to the yard at its east end has been possible since 1970. Dutch-liveried nos. 33103 and 33057 arrive with empty *SEACOWS* from Tonbridge in February 1993. After that time ballast for the Network SouthEast area was obtained by sea from Scotland and in March 1994 the quarry, together with the line as far as the site of Coleford Junction, was sold to ECC Quarries Ltd. Normal departure times for ballast trains on Mondays to Fridays at the end of 1995 were 09.15, 11.42, 14.08, 14.52 and 16.00. (J.A.M.Vaughan)

MELDON VIADUCT

83. The graceful slender lines of this LSWR structure were in great contrast to the massive bulk of the masonry arches to be found extensively on the GWR main line. A staff footbridge also spans the north flowing River Okement. (Lens of Sutton)

84. At a maximum height of 150 ft, the spans are arranged to accommodate the track on a 1 in 77 gradient and 30 chain curve. The Plymouth portion of the 2.50pm from Waterloo is rumbling over at 8.15pm on 6th July 1948. The track was singled between Meldon Quarry and Junction signal boxes on 24th April 1966. (J.H.Aston)

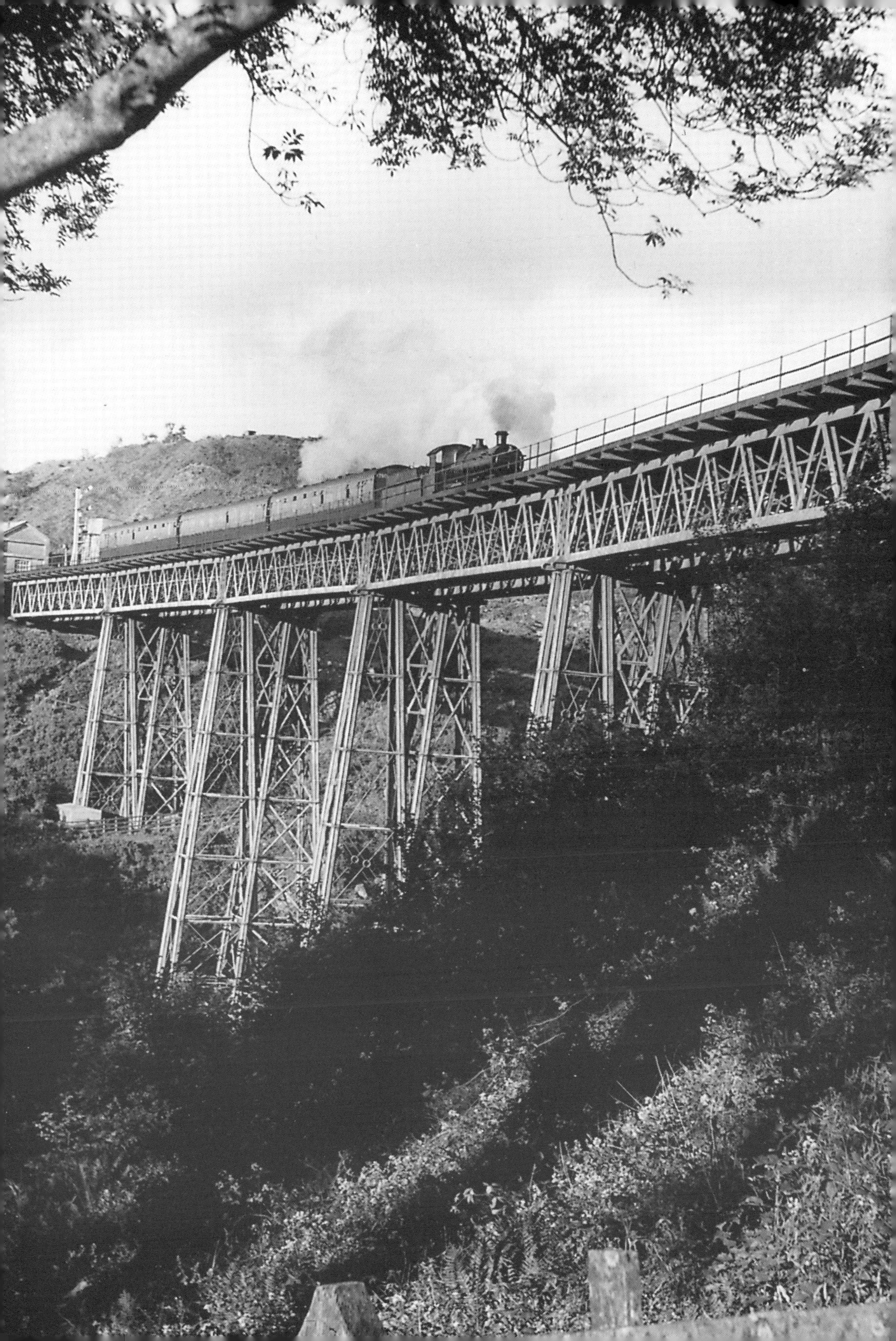

85. The catch points in the foreground are where the climb increases to 1 in 58. No. 34086 *219 Squadron* passes with the 11.15am Waterloo to Plymouth on 26th August 1961. Albeit trackless, the viaduct was still standing in 1995. (S.C.Nash)

MELDON JUNCTION

86. In perfect lighting conditions, class T9 no. 30313 passes over the junction with the North Cornwall Line on 11th May 1961 with the 10.2am Plymouth to Waterloo. The up line was removed in 1964. The ground signal in the left distance was for an up refuge siding; the Bude line is in the right distance. (S.C.Nash)

July 1924

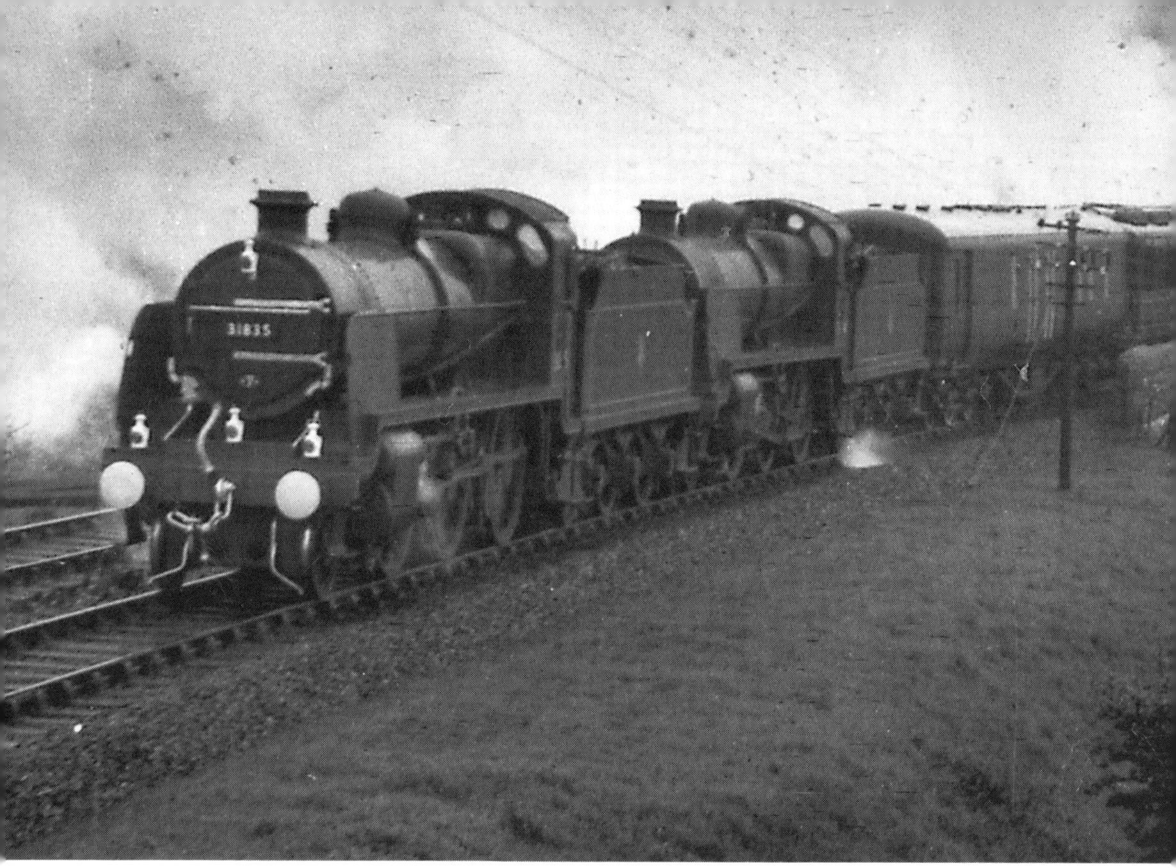
31835

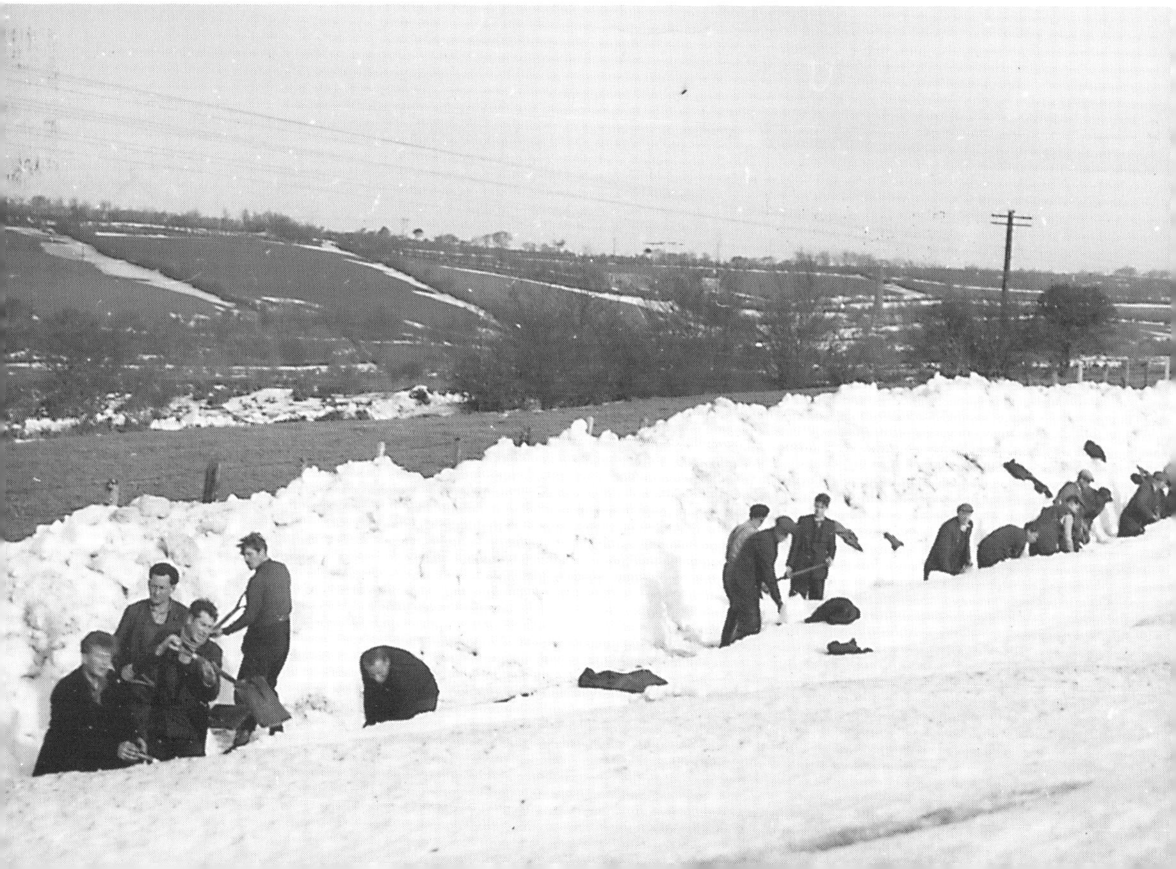

87. In dismal weather on 9th May 1956, the empty Royal Train passes over Lake Viaduct near Sourton, more than two miles south of Meldon Junction. The train was hauled by N class nos. 31835 and 31844 and reversed at Meldon on its journey from Plymouth Millbay to Launceston. (S.C.Nash)

88. Strong winds in blizzards blew the snow off the fields into the cuttings. Clearance is seen on Friday 8th February 1963 as Tuesday's 11.46am Plymouth to Exeter is pulled back from the drift. Attached to it is the engine from the following freight which had gone to its assistance. The Army sent men to help with the rescue. The line reached a height of 960ft above sea level in this vicinity. (R.E.Ruffell)

BRIDESTOWE

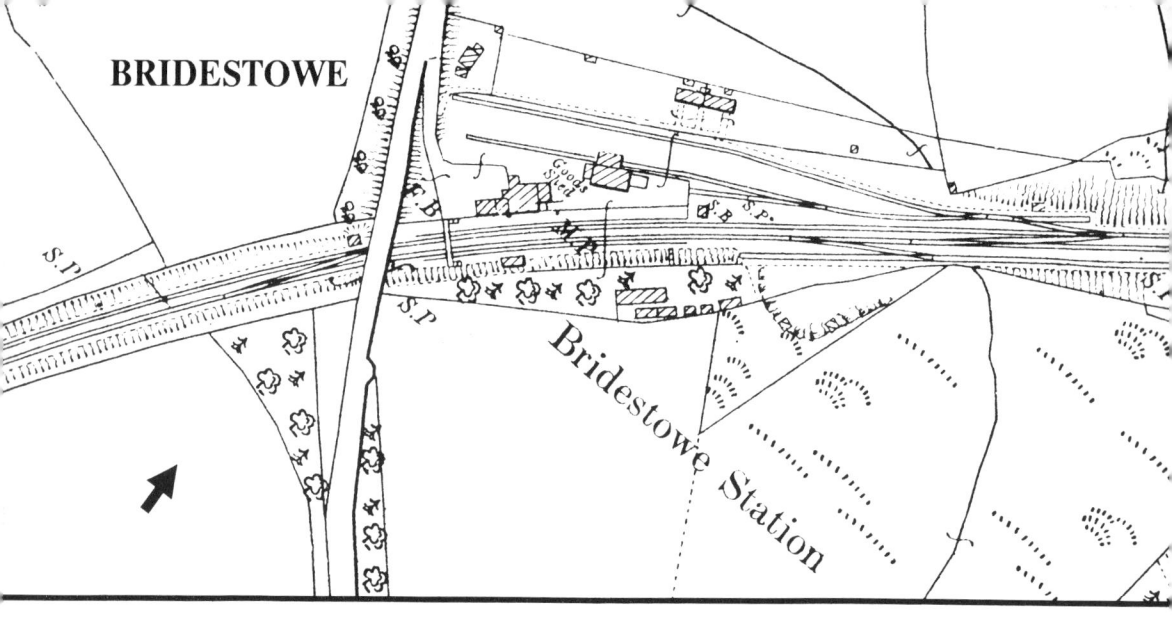

Pronunciation is Brid-ess-toe. The 1906 map shows a layout which changed little during the life of the line. The lower of the three tracks on the right is that of the Rattlebrook Peat Railway.

89. The population of the village dropped from 1049 in 1851 to 457 in 1901; its centre was more than one mile to the north of the station. For decades, the 1.50am Templecombe to Plymouth freight was ordered to pass at 5mph to allow the newspapers to be thrown out. The boxes on this class T9 were for sand and firebox water tubes; the group of engines so fitted had them removed in the 1920s. (Lens of Sutton)

90. A 1955 picture shows the shed at the end of the up platform which served as a booking office. Being close to the signal box, one man could do two jobs. The concrete footbridge had probably replaced the original in the 1930s. The box closed on 14th June 1964. (D.Cullum)

The 1930 map has been enlarged to 2ins to 1 mile to clarify the Rattlebrook Peat Railway. This standard gauge line was opened in 1879 and climbed over 1000ft in its five mile length. Peat was produced for fuel and chemical extraction intermittently and the line was mostly worked by horses. The track was lifted in 1931.

BRIDESTOWE	1928	1936
No. of passenger tickets issued	5712	3342
No. of season tickets issued	39	64
No. of tickets collected	7466	4623
No. of telegrams	636	138
Parcels forwarded	847	205
Parcels received	1029	853
Horses forwarded	27	8
Milk forwarded - cans 1928/gallons 1936	24	-
Milk received - cans 1928/gallons 1936	-	-
General goods forwarded (tons)	116	84
General goods received (tons)	1000	448
Coal, Coke etc. received (tons)	957	779
Other minerals forwarded (tons)	7	24
Other minerals received (tons)	446	256
Trucks livestock forwarded	65	113
Trucks livestock received	11	40
Lavatory pennies	0	175

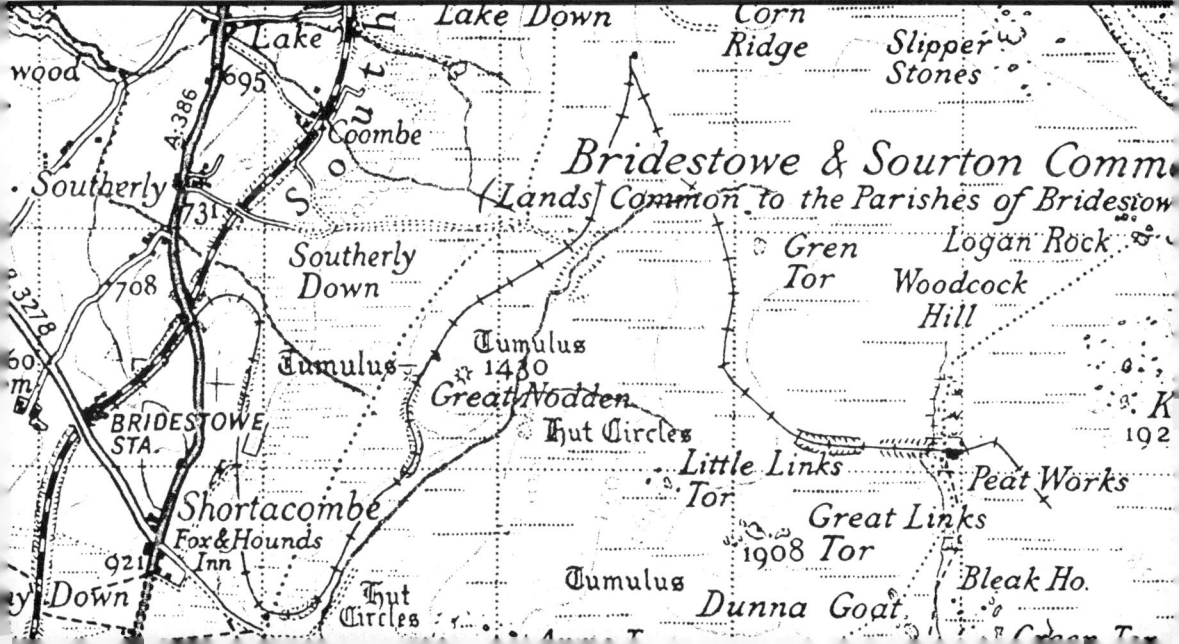

91. A northward view on 7th August 1955 includes much of the goods yard which closed on 5th June 1961. It accommodated a camping coach for some years from 1935. The lower quadrant signals and the signal box probably date from the opening in 1874. (D.Cullum)

92. Cuttings north of the station were still blocked on 8th February 1963. Loads of coal froze solid in wagons and pneumatic drills were used to harvest root vegetables. The next photograph was also taken on the same day. (R.E.Ruffell)

BRIDESTOWE.

Peat works siding.—The private siding which leads to Nodden Gate is operated by the authorities of the Duchy of Cornwall, and wagons containing goods consigned to this siding must be placed immediately beyond the gate and those from the siding must be accepted at that point.

The responsibility for the movement of vehicles over the siding beyond the Company's boundary will rest with the owner of the siding, and in no circumstances must the Company's engine pass beyond the exchange point referred to.

93. Class 700 ex-LSWR 0-6-0 no. 30689 became completely disabled with a cylinder head blown out while exerting herself in a snowdrift. Officially, she had been withdrawn in November 1962, so her fate was sealed in any case. The replacement was seen in picture no. 67. (R.E Ruffell)

94. Staffing ceased on 12th September 1965 but the building was still in use as a dwelling in 1995. The footbridge, goods shed and down platform shelter was also still standing. This picture is probably from 1967. (Wessex coll.)

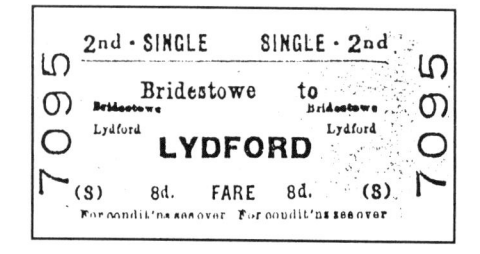

SOUTHERN RAILWAY

Tour East Devon, Dartmoor, The Tamar Valley and Visit North Cornwall

WITH A
7-DAY "HOLIDAY" SEASON

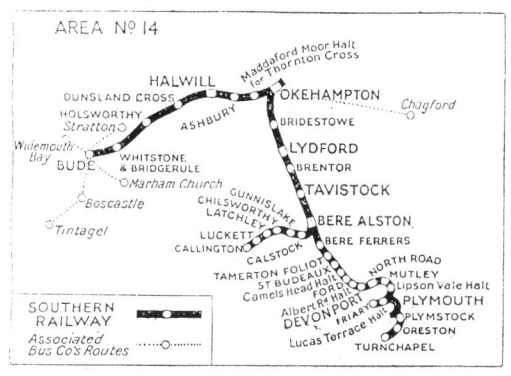

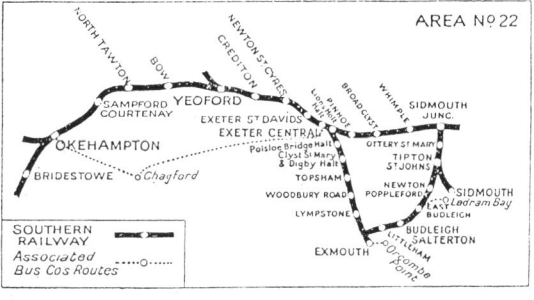

AREA No 14 — Widemouth Bay, Bude, Boscastle, Tintagel, Halwill, Dunsland Cross, Holsworthy, Stratton, Whitstone & Bridgerule, Marham Church, Ashbury, Maddaford Moor Halt (for Thornton Cross), Okehampton, Chagford, Bridestowe, Lydford, Brentor, Gunnislake, Chilsworthy, Latchley, Tavistock, Bere Alston, Bere Ferrers, Luckett, Callington, Calstock, Tamerton Foliot, St Budeaux, Camels Head Halt, Albert Rd Halt, Devonport, Triary, Lucas Terrace Halt, North Road, Mutley, Lipson Vale Halt, Plymouth, Plymstock, Oreston, Turnchapel. SOUTHERN RAILWAY ——●——, Associated Bus Co's Routes ----○----

AREA No 22 — North Tawton, Bow, Sampford Courtenay, Okehampton, Bridestowe, Chagford, Newton St Cyres, Crediton, Yeoford, Exeter St Davids, Exeter Central, Pinhoe, Broadclyst, Whimple, Poltimore Bridge Halt, Clyst St Mary & Digby Halt, Topsham, Woodbury Road, Lympstone, Exmouth, Littleham, Budleigh Salterton, Otterton Point, East Budleigh, Newton Poppleford, Tipton St Johns, Ottery St Mary, Sidmouth Junc., Sidmouth, Ladram Bay. SOUTHERN RAILWAY ——●——, Associated Bus Co's Routes ----○----

The Cheapest Way to Visit the Charming East Devon Resorts, Dartmoor and Tamar Valley Districts, including the North Cornwall Coast

is by using a

10/6
3rd CLASS
each area.

local 7-DAY "HOLIDAY" SEASON, issued DAILY from March 29th until October 31st, 1934, at ANY S.R. STATION shown on the above maps.

15/-
1st CLASS
each area.

The Tickets are available by ANY TRAIN at ANY S.R. STATION in the area, for 7 days, including date of issue.

Fares do not include cost of Road Travel. No allowance or extension of date can be granted on these tickets in consequence of there being no Sunday Service of Trains in certain areas.

CHILDREN UNDER 14—HALF PRICE

Travel WHEN --
WHERE --
and AS OFTEN as you like

Local 7-Day "Holiday" Season Tickets may also be obtained in advance at S.R. London Termini and Agents.
Season Tickets for Dogs and Bicycles accompanying Passengers holding 7-Day "Holiday" Season Tickets are issued at the following charges:—Dog 2/6 per week. Bicycle 5/- per week.
For details of 7-Day "Holiday" Seasons covering other areas, get handbills at the Local S.R. Stations and Offices.

Waterloo Station, S.E. 1.
March, 1934.

H. A. WALKER,
General Manager.

C.X. 459/ 88/12384

Waterlow & Sons Limited, London, Dunstable & Watford.

LYDFORD

The GWR's Launceston to Tavistock 1865 single line runs from the top right. The LSWR 1874 double track from Bridestowe is below it on this 1906 map. Note the common goods shed and cattle pens once used for transfer of traffic between the gauges.

LYDFORD	1928	1936
No. of passenger tickets issued	4606	4089
No. of season tickets issued	12	14
No. of tickets collected	6302	4145
No. of telegrams	1165	855
Parcels forwarded	122	81
Parcels received	245	424
Horses forwarded	27	25
Milk forwarded - cans 1928/gallons 1936	-	-
Milk received - cans 1928/gallons 1936	-	-
General goods forwarded (tons)	6	6
General goods received (tons)	62	35
Coal, Coke etc. received (tons)	31	485
Other minerals forwarded (tons)	61	-
Other minerals received (tons)	30	106
Trucks livestock forwarded	20	9
Trucks livestock received	15	-
Lavatory pennies	180	410

95. Dartmoor is in the background as we look east across the two stations, both trains being on the LSWR route. The GWR signal box is on the right and that of the LSWR on the left; both closed on 31st December 1916 according to the official yellow notice of signal alterations. The village is more than one mile to the north and had around 3000 inhabitants for much of the life of the line.
(Lens of Sutton)

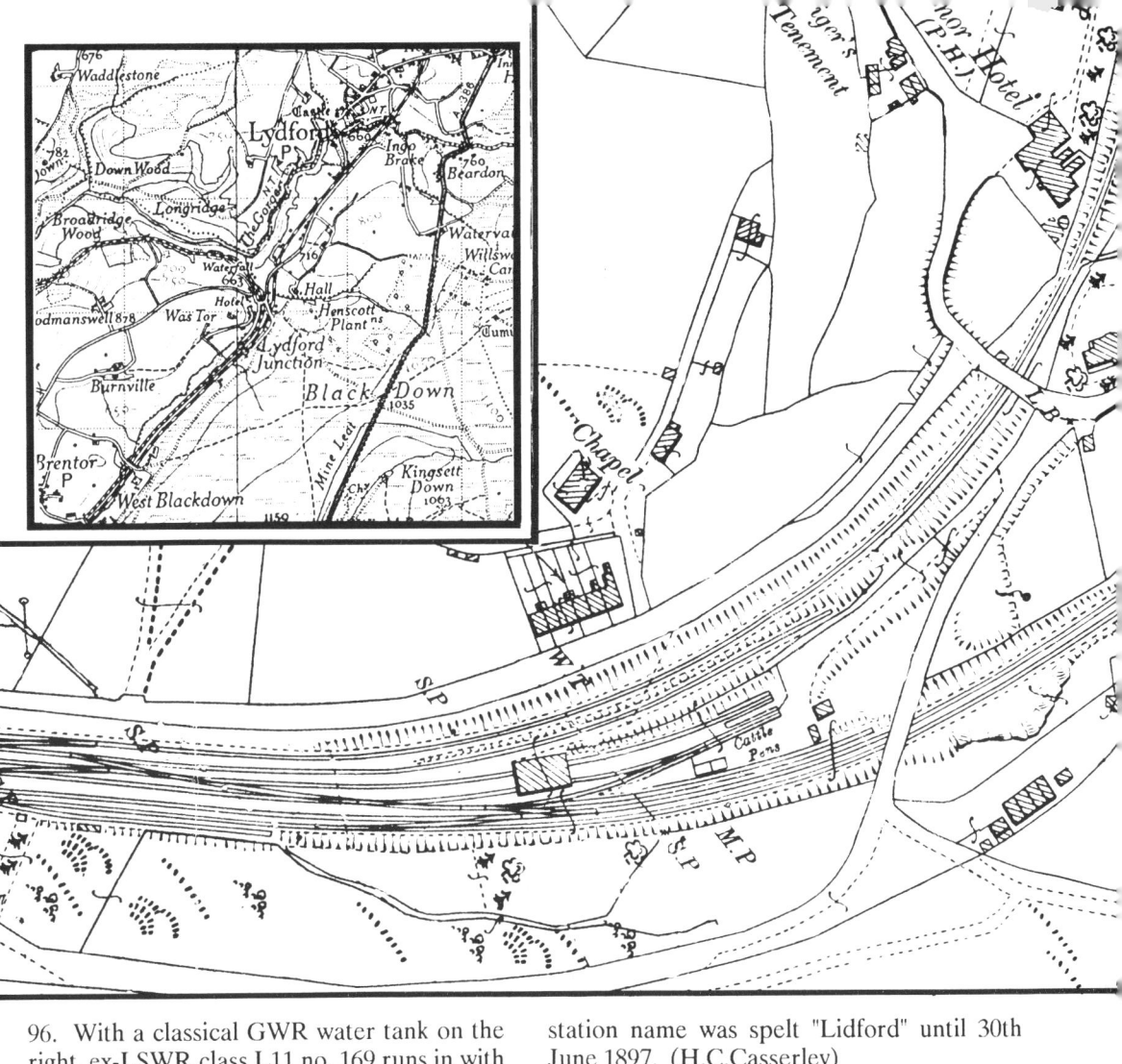

96. With a classical GWR water tank on the right, ex-LSWR class L11 no. 169 runs in with freight from Plymouth on 17th July 1924. The station name was spelt "Lidford" until 30th June 1897. (H.C.Casserley)

97. A southward view from the footbridge in 1955 includes the former LSWR double track to Tavistock (centre) and the connection to the ex-GWR single line to the same town. This link had been disconnected on 19th December 1915 but was reinstated in 1943 when five extra sidings (left) were provided for wartime traffic. The latter resulted in all road traffic having to use the GWR approach road. (D.Cullum)

Rail mounted guns

Massive guns of 9.2, 12, 13.5 and 18 ins bore were in use in Kent in 1940-43 but their graduation (or zeroing) presented a problem in such a populated area. They were therefore brought to Devon for this purpose. The larger guns came complete with their ammunition vans, stores vans, a kitchen car, mess vans, ex-SNCF vans (with bunks for the men) and an officers coach. Each train had its own WD locomotives (usually two ex-GWR 0-6-0 Dean Goods) with Army crews. The SR provided pilotmen, coal and water. The trains were berthed in one of the five sidings east of Lydford station or in the Military Dock at Okehampton. On test day, the gun, together with ammunition and crew vans, was taken onto the Bude branch, about two miles west of Meldon Junction. The rest of the train remained in the siding. Shells were fired to Dartmoor Ranges, four miles distant, although the guns had a range of over 20 miles. More information on these remarkable weapons and their installations can be found in other Middleton Press publications - *Branch Lines around Canterbury* (pictures 104, 105, 108, 109, 110, 113, 116) *Dover to Ramsgate* (32, 33) *Faversham to Dover* (67, 70).

98. Looking north from the same footbridge we witness the arrival of no. 34003 *Plymouth* in 1956. The ends of the 1943 sidings are on the right, while the former goods transfer shed is in the middle. This handled local goods traffic until the yard closed on 7th September 1964. There was only one booking office; it is on the left. (J.W.T.House/C.L.Caddy coll.)

99. The signal box was opened on 31st December 1916 and superseded the separate boxes on the two routes. There were two lever frames, back to back, one for each route. The otherwise separate stations each retained its previous owner's nameboards. No footbridge was provided on the ex-GWR side, which lost its passenger service on 29th December 1962. (Lens of Sutton)

100. Looking north in June 1962, we have the former GWR station on the left and the more generously provided LSWR facilities on the right. The gate on the left was to the original three-siding goods yard. The line through the platform on the left was taken out of use in 1963 but the up line continued to be used by goods trains until 1966. (J.J.Smith)

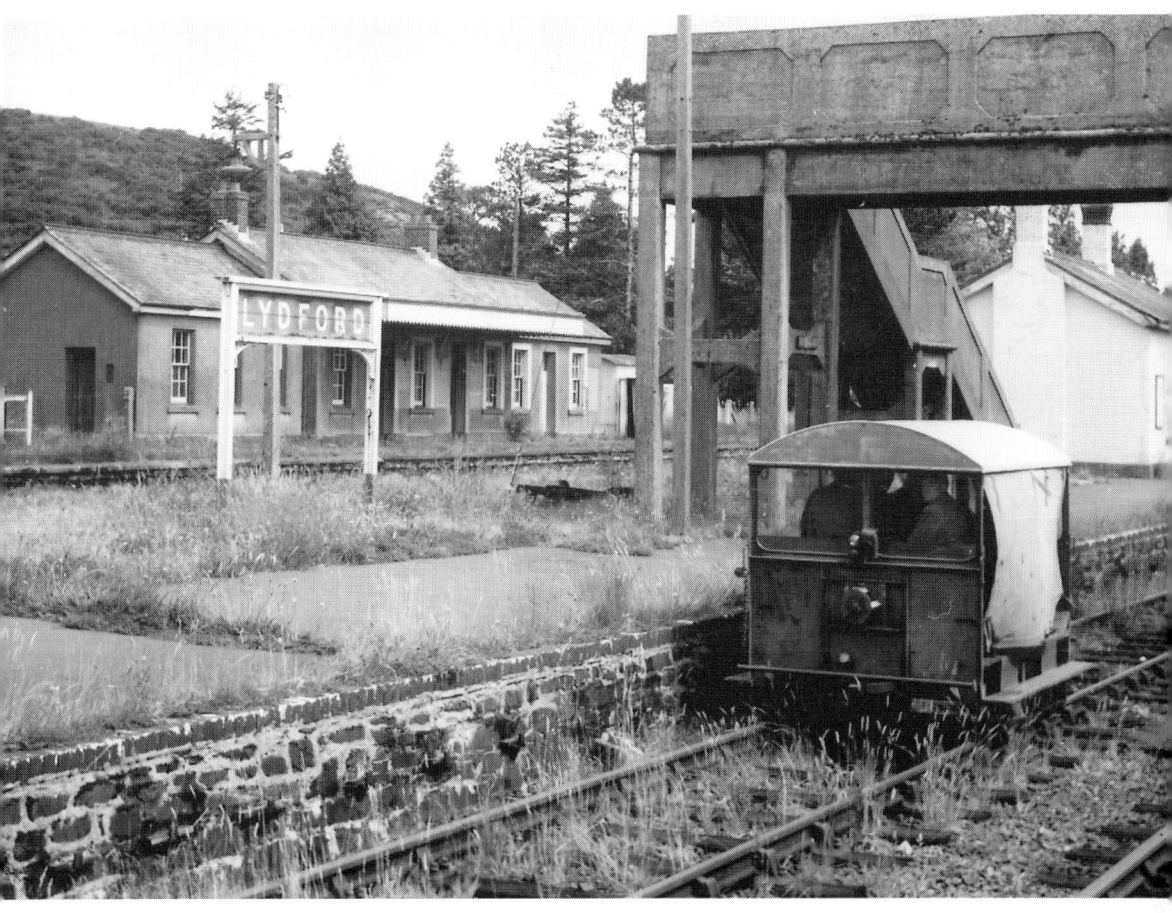

102. Eight officials squeezed into this inspection trolley on 29th July 1969, presumably to plan the demolition of the LSWR's prestigious route from London to Plymouth. Only the nearby railway staff dwellings now remain. (D.J.Aston)

101. Nature was taking over in 1969. The former GWR branch south of Tavistock had been closed completely on 31st December 1962, amidst much confusion due to severe blizzards. North thereof, freight services were operated from Lydford by an engine sent from Okehampton. Until 5th September 1964, it worked south to Tavistock South and north to Lifton (on the Launceston line) but the former closed that day. The line from Lifton to Launceston was reopened for goods trains, as the North Cornwall line lost such facilities. Traffic continued until 28th February 1966. (D.J.Aston)

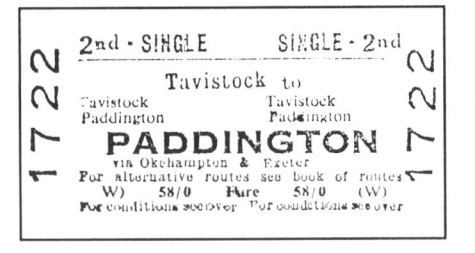

BRENTOR

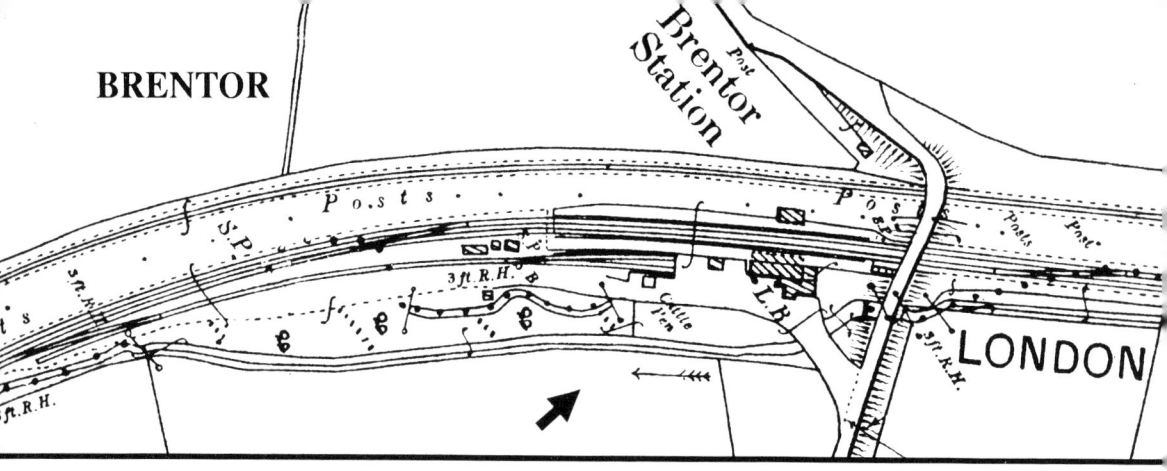

The station was half a mile east of North Brentor which housed only 105 souls in 1901. The GWR single line had no station here but it did have one at Mary Tavy which the LSWR passed by. This was about two miles to the south. The map is from 1905.

BRENTOR	1928	1936
No. of passenger tickets issued	6192	5541
No. of season tickets issued	11	13
No. of tickets collected	7388	7112
No. of telegrams	3	4
Parcels forwarded	149	168
Parcels received	438	444
Horses forwarded	-	1
Milk forwarded - cans 1928/gallons 1936	1046	6737
Milk received - cans 1928/gallons 1936	1	-
General goods forwarded (tons)	29	12
General goods received (tons)	306	24
Coal, Coke etc. received (tons)	270	293
Other minerals forwarded (tons)	-	-
Other minerals received (tons)	121	211
Trucks livestock forwarded	1	1
Trucks livestock received	3	-
Lavatory pennies	0	53

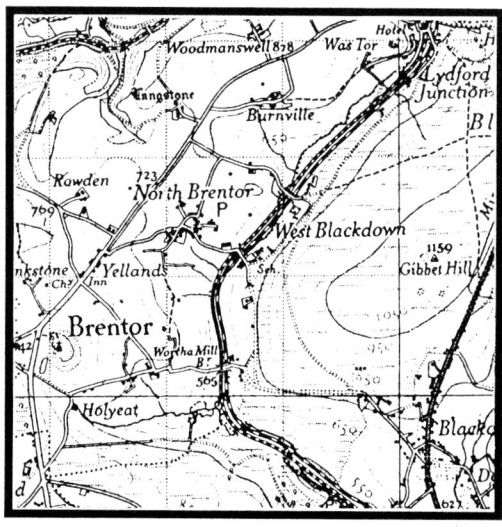

103. The station was built on the side of the valley of the River Burn, at the foot of Dartmoor. On the left are the steps from the down platform up to the road and in the right foreground can be seen the GWR metals. (Lens of Sutton)

104. The route has been troubled by snow blockage many times. This is the problem facing the operators on 26th December 1927. The GWR had the problem of its competing line between Exeter and Plymouth being closed by storms on its coastal section. (H.C.Casserley)

105. Brent Tor is on the left of this 1955 photograph, as is the signal box which closed on 10th June 1961. Goods facilities were withdrawn on 4th April 1960. The fine building was subsequently converted into a desirable residence. (D.Cullum)

106. Rhododendrons adorn the scene on 28th June 1956. The tapered wooden signal posts had been replaced by the SR type made from two old running rails. Class M7 no. 30037 has just run round the 4.5pm from Plymouth Friary which terminated here on weekdays. The train will depart from the down platform at 5.30. (J.H.Aston)

107. The 10.25 Plymouth to Launceston passes by on 23rd June 1962, the last summer of passenger operation. The locomotive is 4500 class no. 4555, more recently to be found working on the Paignton & Dartmouth Steam Railway. (J.J.Smith)

108. Contrasting bridge styles - GWR left and LSWR right. The steps to the up platform were added in about 1920, a useful safety provision in the absence of a footbridge. This is a 1966 view; staffing ceased on 4th September 1967. (Wessex coll.)

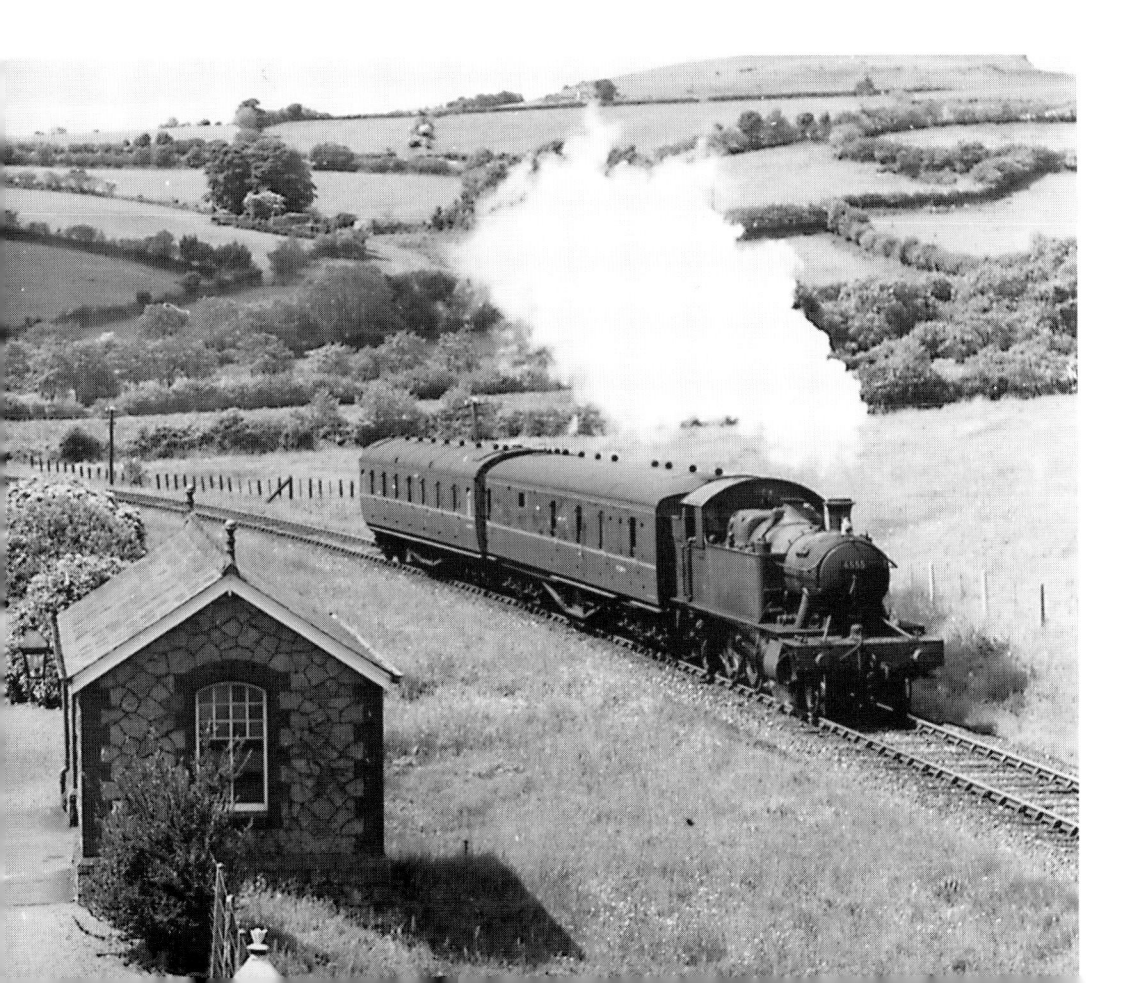

NORTH OF TAVISTOCK

109. The 3.14pm Okehampton to Plymouth (11.0 am ex-Waterloo) was hauled by class N no. 31406 on 6th May 1963. It has just passed over the former GWR Launceston branch, two miles before reaching Tavistock. The two lines ran in close proximity for over six miles. (S.C.Nash)

TAVISTOCK	1928	1936
No. of passenger tickets issued	29162	30820
No. of season tickets issued	250	213
No. of tickets collected	54480	57868
No. of telegrams	4564	4398
Parcels forwarded	2891	2501
Parcels received	5783	5985
Horses forwarded	125	55
Milk forwarded - cans 1928/gallons 1936	6727	50623
Milk received - cans 1928/gallons 1936	108	27
General goods forwarded (tons)	575	466
General goods received (tons)	3667	3482
Coal, Coke etc. received (tons)	1768	3450
Other minerals forwarded (tons)	29829	61821
Other minerals received (tons)	511	8600
Trucks livestock forwarded	612	228
Trucks livestock received	58	27
Lavatory pennies	552	1477

TAVISTOCK NORTH

110. The station was awkwardly situated on a promontory of land between two valleys. This restricted the layout of sidings and made road access difficult; the road to the down side passes under the first arch of the viaduct in this eastward view. (Lens of Sutton)

The 1906 edition has the line from Exeter on the right. The station was about 400ft above sea level but much of the town centre was around 250ft. The crane (Cr.) was of 10-ton capacity.

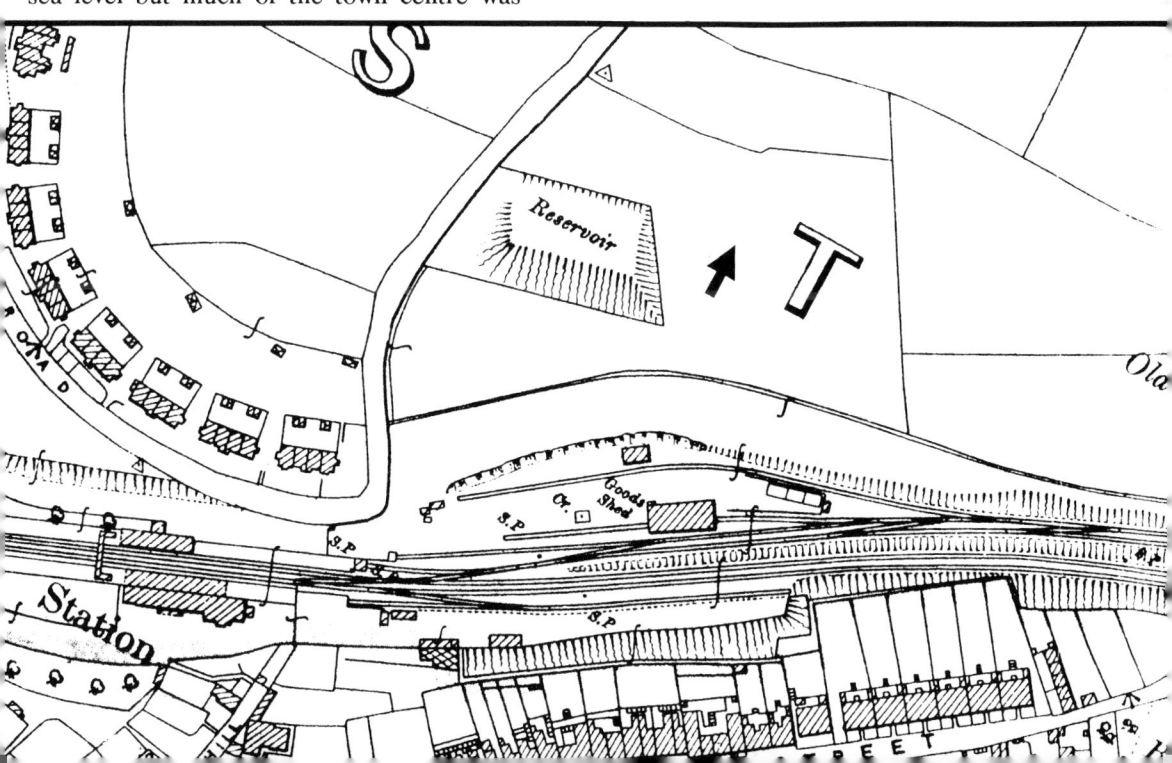

111. One of the successful T9 class arrives at the down platform. Glazing of the footbridge was apparently considered unjustified as there was direct access to both platforms. There were 4728 residents in 1901, this increasing to 6300 in 1961. (Lens of Sutton)

112. The 4.22pm local train from Plymouth Friary terminated at the up platform on 6th May 1939. The locomotive, class T1 0-4-4T no. 5, has run round, moved the train to the down platform and is ready to return to Plymouth. (J.R.W.Kirkby)

113. The single down siding is included in this view towards Brentor. A mile further on, two sidings were provided on the up side at Wilminstone between 1922 and 1955 for Devon County Council. (Lens of Sutton)

114. Class N no. 31833 has propelled its down freight train onto the up line to allow a down passenger service to pass on 28th June 1949. A local train waits in the goods yard. Both the lamp and signal posts are of concrete. (J.H.Aston)

115. The suffix "North" was added by the newly formed BR on 26th September 1949. The south crossover is on the viaduct; the latter was still standing in 1996. The down side buildings were in residential use. (D.Cullum)

116. This and the previous picture were taken from the footbridge on 7th August 1955. Stock for a local train working to Plymouth is in the distance. Such trains departed at 6.0, 7.20am, 4.20, 6.55 and 8.20pm on weekdays. Another started back from Brentor at 5.30pm. (D.Cullum)

117. The exterior of the down side buildings was recorded in September 1957. The approach would be particularly busy with the arrival of the "Atlantic Coast Express" at 3.47pm. It left Waterloo at 11.0am with through coaches for Padstow, Bude, Plymouth, Ilfracombe, Torrington, Exmouth and Sidmouth. (Lens of Sutton)

TAVISTOCK.

Wilminstone Quarry.—Blasting operations are frequently carried out at this quarry, and Drivers must keep a good look-out and be prepared to stop in response to any hand signals that may be exhibited.

Wilminstone siding (Devon County Council).—A refuge siding of sufficient length to accommodate a train of 25 goods wagons, including van, is provided on the Company's property. A connection has been made from this siding to another siding leading into the Devon County Council's stone quarries, the points of which are facing for trains shunting from the direction of the main line. A hopper is provided in this siding for the purpose of loading wagons with stone.

The points at the siding end of the main line connection lead also to a short catch road.

Before the work of attaching or detaching wagons at the siding is commenced, the train must be shunted into the refuge siding. Under no circumstances must any vehicle be left standing on the main line.

Vehicles for the siding must be placed in the County Council siding, and left at a point beyond the gate clear of the refuge siding. Those from the siding must be accepted at that point, and care must be taken to see that no vehicle is left standing foul of the refuge siding.

A competent man from Tavistock will assist with the working.

Traffic for down line stations must circulate via Lydford.

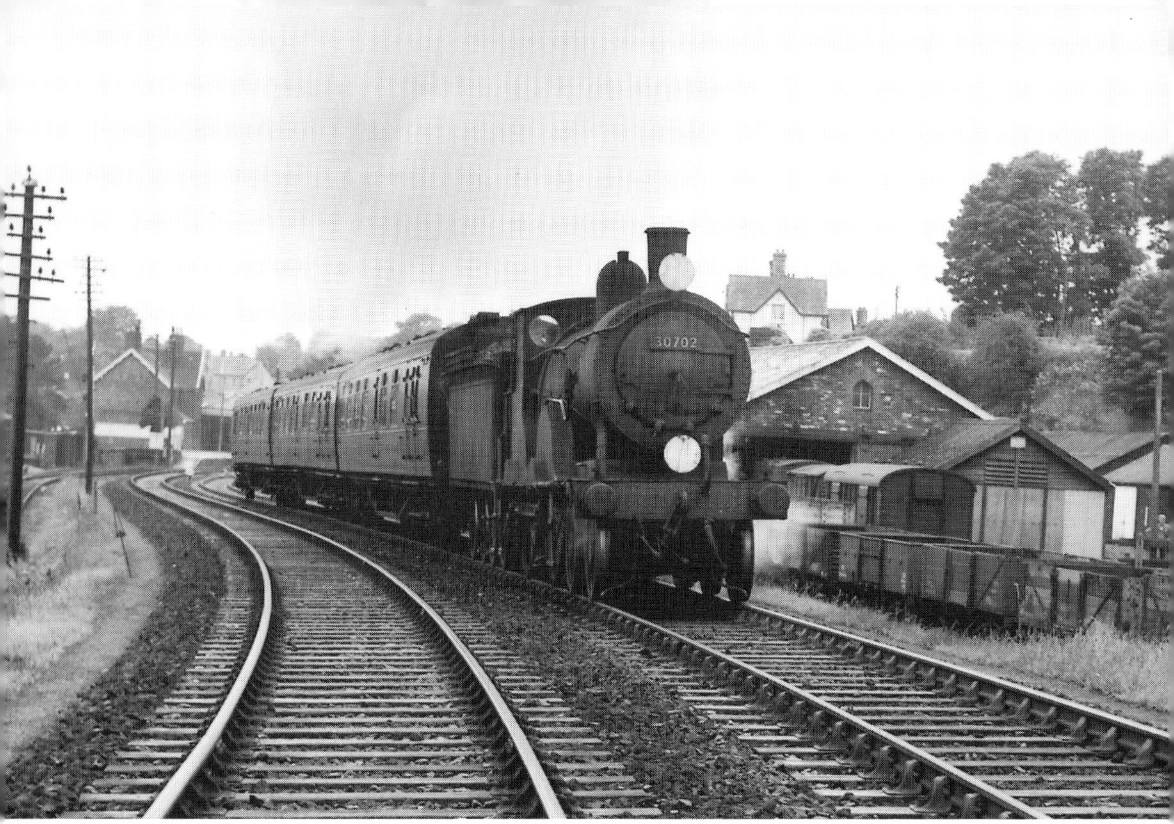

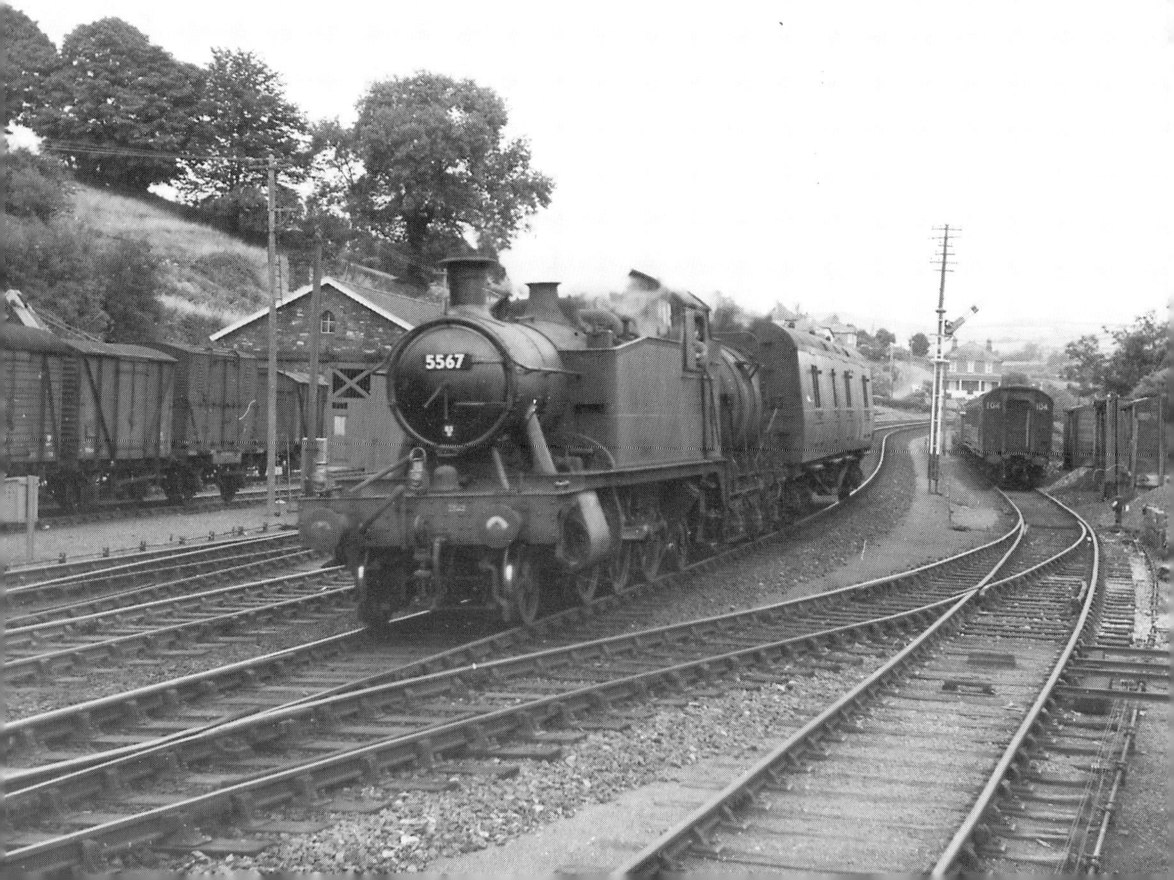

118. The Plymouth portion of the up "ACE" leaves at 10.35am on 5th June 1959 behind class T9 no. 30702. It would join the Padstow and Bude coaches at Okehampton. The next up departure was the 11.41 through train to Brighton, arrival there being due at 5.22pm. (J.H.Aston)

119. Ex-GWR 2-6-2T no. 5567 drifts down the 1 in 75 gradient with a milk train on 19th July 1959. The goods yard closed on 28th February 1966, the ex-GWR yard having succumbed on 7th September 1964. (Wessex coll.)

120. The signal box remained open until the station closed completely on 6th May 1968. No. D851 arrives with the 10.25 Brighton to Plymouth on 3rd October 1964. Despite the economies that dieselisation brought, this unique scenic route sadly fell under the "Beeching Axe". (C.L.Caddy)

MP Middleton Press

Easebourne Lane, Midhurst. West Sussex. GU29 9AZ Tel: 01730 813169 Fax: 01730 812601
..... Write or telephone for our latest list .....

BRANCH LINES
Branch Line to Allhallows
Branch Lines to Alton
Branch Lines around Ascot
Branch Line to Bude
Branch Lines around Canterbury
Branch Lines to East Grinstead
Branch Lines around Effingham Jn
Branch Lines to Exmouth
Branch Line to Fairford
Branch Line to Hawkhurst
Branch Lines to Horsham
Branch Lines around Huntingdon
Branch Lines to Ilfracombe
Branch Line to Lyme Regis
Branch Line to Lynton
Branch Lines around March
Branch Lines around Midhurst
Branch Lines to Newport
Branch Line to Padstow
Branch Lines around Portmadoc 1923-46
Branch Lines around Porthmadog 1954-94
Branch Lines to Seaton & Sidmouth
Branch Line to Selsey
Branch Lines around Sheerness
Branch Line to Southwold
Branch Line to Swanage
Branch Line to Tenterden
Branch Lines to Torrington
Branch Lines to Tunbridge Wells
Branch Line to Upwell
Branch Lines around Weymouth

LONDON SUBURBAN RAILWAYS
Caterham and Tattenham Corner
Clapham Jn. to Beckenham Jn.
Crystal Palace and Catford Loop
Holborn Viaduct to Lewisham
London Bridge to Addiscombe
Mitcham Junction Lines
South London Line
West Croydon to Epsom
Wimbledon to Epsom

STEAMING THROUGH
Steaming through Cornwall
Steaming through East Sussex
Steaming through the Isle of Wight
Steaming through Surrey
Steaming through West Hants
Steaming through West Sussex

GREAT RAILWAY ERAS
Ashford from Steam to Eurostar

COUNTRY BOOKS
Brickmaking in Sussex
East Grinstead Then and Now

SOUTH COAST RAILWAYS
Ashford to Dover
Bournemouth to Weymouth
Brighton to Eastbourne
Brighton to Worthing
Chichester to Portsmouth
Dover to Ramsgate
Hastings to Ashford
Ryde to Ventnor
Worthing to Chichester

SOUTHERN MAIN LINES
Bromley South to Rochester
Charing Cross to Orpington
Crawley to Littlehampton
Dartford to Sittingbourne
East Croydon to Three Bridges
Epsom to Horsham
Exeter to Barnstaple
Exeter to Tavistock
Faversham to Dover
Haywards Heath to Seaford
London Bridge to East Croydon
Orpington to Tonbridge
Sittingbourne to Ramsgate
Swanley to Ashford
Three Bridges to Brighton
Tonbridge to Hastings
Victoria to Bromley South
Waterloo to Windsor
Woking to Southampton
Yeovil to Exeter

COUNTRY RAILWAY ROUTES
Andover to Southampton
Bath to Evercreech Junction
Bournemouth to Evercreech Jn
Burnham to Evercreech Junction
Croydon to East Grinstead
East Kent Light Railway
Fareham to Salisbury
Guildford to Redhill
Porthmadog to Blaenau
Reading to Basingstoke
Reading to Guildford
Redhill to Ashford
Salisbury to Westbury
Strood to Paddock Wood
Taunton to Barnstaple
Westbury to Bath
Woking to Alton

TROLLEYBUS CLASSICS
Woolwich & Dartford Trolleybuses

TRAMWAY CLASSICS
Aldgate & Stepney Tramways
Bournemouth & Poole Tramways
Brighton's Tramways
Bristol's Tramways
Camberwell & W. Norwood Tramways
Croydon's Tramways
Dover's Tramways
East Ham & West Ham Tramways
Embankment & Waterloo Tramways
Exeter & Taunton Tramways
Greenwich & Dartford Tramways
Hampstead & Highgate Tramways
Hastings Tramways
Ilford & Barking Tramways
Kingston & Wimbledon Tramways
Lewisham & Catford Tramways
Maidstone & Chatham Tramways
North Kent Tramways
Southampton Tramways
Southend-on-sea Tramways
Thanet's Tramways
Victoria & Lambeth Tramways
Walthamstow & Leyton Tramways
Wandsworth & Battersea Tramways

OTHER RAILWAY BOOKS
Garraway Father & Son
Industrial Railways of the South East
London Chatham & Dover Railway
South Eastern Railway
War on the Line

MILITARY BOOKS
Battle over Portsmouth
Battle Over Sussex 1940
Blitz Over Sussex 1941-42
Bognor at War
Bombers over Sussex 1943-45
Military Defence of West Sussex

WATERWAY ALBUMS
Hampshire Waterways
Kent and East Sussex Waterways
London to Portsmouth Waterway
West Sussex Waterways

BUS BOOK
Eastbourne Bus Story

SOUTHERN RAILWAY
● VIDEOS ●
Memories of the Hayling Island Branch
Memories of the Lyme Regis Branch
War on the Line